GETTING THE MOST FROM

Professional Handbooks in Counselling and Psychotherapy

This series of professional handbooks is designed for trainees as well as practitioners in the field of psychological therapy, counselling, emotional wellbeing and mental health. It focuses on key areas of practice interest and training need.

The books are characterised by:

- their pluralistic and undogmatic approach to theory – theoretically informed, they maintain a flexible view about what works for whom
- their practical stance – the books all focus on the guidance professionals need in order to optimise their skills and effectiveness
- their easy-to-use format – they are clearly structured in order to aid navigation and employ devices such as vignettes, transcripts, checklists and reflective questions to support the reader in deepening their understanding of the main issues.

Published

Robert Bor, Sheila Gill, Riva Miller and Amanda Evens
Counselling in Health Care Settings: A Handbook for Practitioners

Robert Bor and Anne Stokes
Setting Up in Independent Practice: A Handbook for Therapy and Psychology Practitioners

Susy Churchill
The Troubled Mind: A Handbook of Therapeutic Approaches to Psychological Distress

Alan Dunnett, Caroline Jesper, Máire O'Donnell and Kate Vallance
Getting the Most from Supervision: A Guide for Counsellors and Psychotherapists

Gill Jones and Anne Stokes
Online Counselling: A Handbook for Practitioners

Maxine Rosenfield
Telephone Counselling

Getting the Most from Supervision

A Guide for Counsellors and Psychotherapists

Alan Dunnett
Caroline Jesper
Máire O'Donnell
Kate Vallance

Dear Steven, enormous thanks for all your support through the ups and downs of this writy enterprise.

palgrave
macmillan

Much love Kate Vallance

© Alan Dunnett, Caroline Jesper, Máire O'Donnell and Kate Vallance 2013

First published 2013 by
PALGRAVE MACMILLAN

Palgrave Macmillan in the UK is an imprint of Macmillan Publishers Limited,
registered in England, company number 785998, of Houndmills, Basingstoke,
Hampshire RG21 6XS.

Palgrave Macmillan in the US is a division of St Martin's Press LLC,
175 Fifth Avenue, New York, NY 10010.

Palgrave Macmillan is the global academic imprint of the above companies
and has companies and representatives throughout the world.

Palgrave® and Macmillan® are registered trademarks in the United States,
the United Kingdom, Europe and other countries

ISBN: 978-0-230-34834-9

This book is printed on paper suitable for recycling and made from fully
managed and sustained forest sources. Logging, pulping and manufacturing
processes are expected to conform to the environmental regulations of the
country of origin.

A catalogue record for this book is available from the British Library.

A catalog record for this book is available from the Library of Congress.

Printed in China

Contents

Boxes, tables and figures

FIGURES

Preface

The growing importance of counsellors and psychotherapists in the promotion of good mental health and well-being has begun to provide for many people possibilities of access to a new source of support and personal development. Very reasonably, governments and organizations ask increasingly searching questions of the professionals responsible for its delivery – questions which aim to clarify the status and validity of qualifications and experience. The demand from these bodies is that competence be convincingly demonstrated, standards of practice evidenced, and that practitioners' knowledge be updated against current theory and research.

The approaches to supervision adopted in the UK and widely shared internationally address these needs, and aspire to facilitate the professional development of the multiplicity of practitioners across the whole range of practice settings. The ubiquity of the requirement for supervision means that most – and, over time, all – of those involved in the counselling and psychotherapy professions will be touched by its impact. Supervision, then, becomes a necessary and appropriate preoccupation for those delivering psychotherapeutic services.

This book adds to a growing literature on supervision by examining the experience of the supervisee. Whilst therapists at different stages of their career may find themselves heading for particular sections, each chapter is addressed to the profession as a whole and takes account of questions and concerns common to us all. The book's intention is to explicate, for the therapist in the early months of practice, the mechanics and utility of the process. For practitioners with more experience, it invites a review of the ways in which supervision is being used, the roles of the parties involved, and the possibilities for optimizing the activity. For those in the mature years of practice, it offers an opportunity to renew a commitment to supervision by focusing on key aspects of the dynamic, and on the advantages and dilemmas posed by the long-term supervisory relationship. The explorations of ethical issues and of the place of technologically-based, group and creative approaches are likely, at some point, to be relevant to the needs of all supervisees.

As authors, we are all experienced supervisors. As counsellors in a range of therapeutic settings, we are also supervisees ourselves and have been supervised throughout our many years of practice. We recognize the dilemmas which may arise in selecting and developing a relationship with a supervisor. The issues and dynamics which we write about have all figured in some way in our own lives as supervisees. Just as we are familiar with the challenges, so we appreciate the manifold benefits of supervision when it is working effectively. We acknowledge the significance of the individual context and of the need for pragmatism. Our aim is to promote the kind of reflexive practice which monitors the nature and impact of supervision, is proactive in harnessing and influencing the process, and, above all, ensures that therapeutic practice is reliably supported.

The four authors share a belief in the transformative potential of supervision. The humanistic principles of self-direction and autonomy are central to the philosophy underpinning the chapters. Practitioners are to be trusted to develop and work with integrity. We argue not for more rules, but for interactions in supervision which facilitate therapists to take full responsibility for their work and to be capable of giving account for their choices – to themselves and to other stakeholders. In so doing, we recognize possible areas of conflict with elements of the mainstream culture which emphasize the primacy of external command and control.

The genesis of this book has common ground with the development of relationships in a supervision group: four individuals discovering how to work together on an agreed commitment, sharing sometimes complementary, sometimes divergent perspectives, challenging and being challenged, stimulating collective understandings and energy for the task. Vulnerabilities and anxiety have been, for the authors, as much a part of the mix as excitement and satisfaction. The giving and receiving of feedback has had to be negotiated. Multiple roles have had to be managed. With time has come more trust in ourselves and the process. The content of the 10 chapters likewise parallels the supervision process itself, acknowledging the uniqueness of each supervisory dyad and recognizing that no universal panacea exists.

In the text, the terms *supervisee, counsellor, practitioner* and *therapist* are used interchangeably. The same applies to the use of the pronouns he/she: no gender bias is intended.

Above all, this book is intended to invigorate and encourage. The supervision process can sometimes be experienced as a burden or a drudge. Since our experience has often been very different from that, our aspiration is to infuse supervisees with enthusiasm for what can be a highly influential and consistently rewarding part of professional life.

AD/CJ/MO'D/KV
North Yorkshire
March 2013

Acknowledgements

We wish to acknowledge the debt we owe to each and every supervisee and supervisor we have encountered throughout our years of practice without whom our learning would have had less depth and breadth. Thank you for your understanding and patience as we developed our appreciation of what constitutes becoming knowledgeable, facilitative and hopefully insightful supervisees and supervisors.

Most especially we wish to thank our families, friends and colleagues for their support throughout the writing of this book, and Sue Vincent for her advice on managing, coping with four authors, and many other areas of publishing and editing.

We are indebted to OH-Publishing for granting permission to reproduce images from their cards.

Finally we thank Catherine Gray, our editor at Palgrave Macmillan, for her support, guidance and encouragement throughout the project and for bringing the book to fruition.

Chapter 1

Setting the Scene

INTRODUCTIONS

> **Supervisor**: Welcome, Sarah. You found the place alright.
>
> **Sarah**: No problem. It's easy to find.
>
> **Supervisor**: I expect we both have ideas about what we want from today. Would you like to start or shall I?
>
> **Sarah**: Perhaps I'll start by giving you a bit of background to my contacting you (…)

How to begin any professional relationship? A working alliance between supervisee and supervisor has to start somewhere – and is best undertaken with an adequate amount of sharing of relevant information. Introductory sessions can be a vital source of indicators for both parties as to whether or not this crucial component of professional activity will be effective. Undeniably, anxieties will be present on both sides: counsellor and supervisor are on show and are being judged. Planning for the session – deciding what it is you would like to communicate and to find out – can help alleviate the pressure of a first meeting.

Before we go further in this book, and in the spirit of transparency, it is important to declare who we as authors are and the position from which we are writing. Whilst you the reader are not, of course, engaging any of us in the role of supervisor, it may inform your expectations of the pages that follow if we explain a little about our theoretical backgrounds and values.

All four authors have trained in a humanistic-integrative model of counselling and each of us has developed that theoretical position in her or his own way over the years. The basic humanistic values underpin all of our work and beliefs about therapy, with strong support from the person-

1

centred tradition. The influences which each of us have combined with that foundation are varied, though the power of the therapeutic relationship is a consistent thread, as is the belief in maintaining a safe and psychologically contained space within which personal growth and restorative activity can occur. We acknowledge the significance of systems within which people live their lives (families and friends, work and leisure, communities and the wider society). We recognize the connections between the elements of our personal worlds – physical and mental health, the intellect and the emotions, the ways we connect with others and ourselves. Humankind, we know, is both boundaried and energized by the existential givens that we share with each other.

In purely practical ways, we have followed different pathways to where we have arrived as therapists and supervisors. Kate's background is as a manager in industry, consultant, coach and mentor, and she continues to pursue these latter roles alongside her therapeutic practice. Caroline's experience is in counselling and supervision within education, the UK's National Health Service (NHS) and the voluntary and private sector. She is currently the course director of a postgraduate supervisor training programme. Alan's years as a college and university lecturer span more than four decades, initially as a tutor in modern languages and later leading a teaching team in counselling. Máire is a supervisor and counsellor, and a consultant and trainer to small voluntary organizations and self-help groups. Her previous career was in nursing and hospice management. These disparate experiences inevitably colour and combine with what we have learned in the world of therapy. Since we advocate autonomous thinking and shun the idea of prescription, what follows are intended as invitations to reflection about what works in the supervisory space. In this, we aspire to echo in the book the style of interaction with you, the reader, which we believe to be effective between supervisor and supervisee.

WHAT IS SUPERVISION?

> Joe has recently enrolled on a counselling course and has been told to get himself a supervisor from the course list. Dutifully he has selected and met with Diane. She seemed like a pleasant enough person. However, he is left with a nagging doubt as to what exactly they are to do together. She appears to expect him to take the lead outlining his hopes and expectations and frankly he is really unsure of the rationale for, or purpose of, their relationship.

The concept of supervision is based on a range of precedents, which go well beyond the notion of (literally) 'over-seeing' the work of a counsellor. Many professionals in caring and health-related roles and in social work have long been familiar with the idea of a senior practitioner guiding and supporting the activity of less experienced colleagues.

Fundamentally, the definition employed by this book begins with the assumption that two or more practitioners (counsellors or psychotherapists) meet on a regular basis to discuss aspects of therapeutic practice. One of the practitioners provides facilitation to the other(s), whose role is to learn, monitor and develop their competence.

Drawn on this barest of outlines are a number of more closely defined features which, taken together, give counsellor supervision its particular character.

First, the process is clearly educative – almost along the lines of some kinds of teacher education, in that facilitators are themselves being facilitated. The distinction from teacher education is that counsellor supervision as an activity does not have a fixed curriculum and does not work to specifically stated outcomes.

Second, supervision obviously *does* work towards a 'spread effect'. Counsellors attend not just because they are required to do so (as indeed is the case with many professional affiliations in the UK), but because they aspire to deeper understanding and greater effectiveness. Ultimately, the practitioner's current and future clients should be the beneficiaries.

The place and space of supervision encourages in-depth reflection and sponsors the harnessing of creative processes. The physical location must be conducive to this kind of meeting: a noisy cafe table will not do. As to the kind of processes which are in play, right-brain functions – free association, imagination, intuition – are just as important as logic and reason. A certain kind of thinking develops, based in dialogue and in the willingness to consider what may lie at the edge of awareness and of possibility.

Supervision has been called 'an intensive, interpersonally focussed' interaction (Loganbill et al., 1982), quite unlike any other relationship. Uniquely, it harnesses not just the supervisee's experience of the client and themselves in the therapy space, but also the 'out-there' material from the personal and professional lives of supervisor and supervisee, as well as the 'in the room' relationship between the two practitioners in conversation. This wealth of material gives unlimited scope for exploration (Gilbert & Evans, 2000; Hawkins & Shohet, 2012; Henderson, 2009).

To add the final – and crucial – brush strokes to this portrait, supervision presents a forum in which counsellors offer account of themselves: this, in order to assure themselves and anyone else who needs them to be account-able that they are practising responsibly. Ethical mindfulness, which in this description is presented as the finishing touch, is in truth the signature without which supervision cannot be seen as valid and valuable.

COUNSELLING AND PSYCHOTHERAPY

A debate which has preoccupied the profession for decades concerns dif-ferent interpretations of what constitutes the practice of counselling and of psychotherapy. The psychotherapy community points to the long initial training period (four or more years), to the requirement for regular personal therapy, and to high numbers of obligatory practice hours prior to qualifi-cation. In some definitions of psychotherapy, there are references to 'working at depth', or to a particular therapeutic orientation requiring longer intervention (such as some forms of psychodynamic psychotherapy), or to working with individuals with more serious and entrenched mental health problems. The training of psychotherapists in the UK is rarer than that of counsellors by a factor of at least 10, with fewer than 500 currently registered students at first degree or (mostly) postgraduate level. This sector is nonetheless sometimes perceived as more status-rich than the counselling sector, with a salary differential to match.

One of the barriers to definition of the term 'counselling' derives from the very wide range of levels, standards and approaches which characterize the field of training, making generalizations well-nigh impossible. Three factors, already appearing on the scene, are likely to bring change. In the first place, professional registration will increasingly influence entry to employment, requiring minimum levels of qualification and competence. Second, UK national benchmarking standards will apply only to those train-ing programmes operating at least at the level of a first degree – a BA/BSc (Hons) in Counselling. Third, the likelihood is that the number, spread and diversity of training courses will change in response to political and eco-nomic factors, including funding models in education and patterns of coun-sellor employment.

Published definitions of psychotherapy and counselling can be helpful in providing details of the nature and purpose of the activity, but do not necessarily assist in determining the differences between these terms. The United Kingdom Council for Psychotherapy (UKCP) has defined psychotherapy as 'one of the "talking therapies". It can help people gain insight into their difficulties or distress, establish a greater under-standing of their motivation, enable them to find more appropriate ways of coping and bring about changes in their thinking and behaviour' (UKCP, 2012).

A briefing from BACP, the largest UK organization representing both counsellors and psychotherapists, states: 'Counselling and psychotherapy are umbrella terms that cover a range of talking therapies. They are delivered by trained practitioners who work with people over the short or long term to help them bring about effective change and enhance their well-being. Counselling and psychotherapy can be hugely beneficial for many people in a wide variety of situations including helping people to cope with depression and anxiety, bereavement, relationship difficulties, sexual and racial issues, child abuse and educational dilemmas, as well as personal problem solving. Therapy offers people a safe, confidential place to talk about life issues and problems that may be confusing, painful or uncomfortable' (BACP, 2012a).

Whilst the boundary between the service delivered by counsellors and that delivered by psychotherapists may be hard to define, there are many in the profession for whom a significant differential is held to exist between the two descriptors of psychotherapeutic activity. Initial training, employer preference and the perceptions of the client group can all be influential in determining the shape of the distinction. The point for the purposes of this book is not whether the differentiation is real or perceived, but the extent to which perceptions of the terms might influence the supervision arrangement. The following questions may serve to prompt reflection:

For Reflection

- Do you draw a distinction between 'counselling' and 'psychotherapy' – and if so in what way?
- Is it important to you to work with a supervisor who uses the same professional title ('counsellor' or 'psychotherapist') as yourself?
- What problems could you foresee if supervisee and supervisor have diverging interpretations of these terms?

WHY SUPERVISION?

The emergence of any professional activity not sanctified by a long history of practice is inevitably accompanied by the need to justify its presence. Taking the adjacent example of professionals in the treatment of physical health – doctors, nurses, physiotherapists – if there is no requirement on these individuals to access regular supervision, why should it be different for counsellors? Isn't it enough to take a responsible position towards reading, updating and continuing professional development?

The responses to this challenge rely on an understanding of the complex intra- and interpersonal dynamics involved in the psychotherapies. Many psychotherapeutic interventions are predicated on a highly individualized relationship between client and practitioner, often and at best involving a significant level of psychological contact. The unique character of each and every therapeutic encounter removes the option of a standardized set of procedures and obliges the counsellor/psychotherapist to be consistently self-aware, reflexive and creative. Whilst it would be expected that the more mature practitioner can ask him or herself many key questions pertaining to a particular interaction, even the most experienced is not immune to developing blind spots, stuckness and confusion about the process. Supervision serves as consultancy – supportive, challenging and educative – to the whole range of providers in whatever branch of the profession.

> Beth worked both as a teacher and a part-time counsellor in a large inner city comprehensive school. She had become used to a regime of over-work, often squeezing in counselling sessions between lessons and meetings. She knew that she should be supervised for her counselling, but never found the time, reassuring herself that she had worked with teenage children for 10 years and knew how they operated. One day, a troubled 16-year-old whom she had been seeing for counselling attempted to kiss her as he was leaving the room. Although managing to resist his advances, she struggled to cope with the impact of the event and did not know who to talk to or how to proceed. She was fearful that this event would become public knowledge and that she would lose her job.

Beth's experience illustrates one of the countless variety of unexpected events which can occur in counselling, and the isolation which can ensue from working unsupervised. It could be argued that, had she had a regular opportunity to review her practice, she could have explored subtleties in this and other counselling relationships, increased her awareness, and planned strategies in the case of aggressive behaviour or sexual advances. Just as important, she would have had an immediate resource for debriefing and support through a taxing time in her life.

It may be that a counsellor's agency or employer will be sensitized to the need to provide supervision, though there are plenty of situations where it is necessary to argue for its utility. The reasons generally advanced for supervision include:

- enhancements to counsellor confidence and effectiveness through increased self-awareness and more consistent application of skills and knowledge
- provision of a safe space for reflection on issues and dilemmas
- ethical safeguarding – supervision assists the individual and the organization to ensure that the service provided meets published norms and standards
- health and safety of the lone worker – supervision supports the counsellor in what is essentially a solitary activity, enhancing the well-being of the service provider and the service user
- continuing professional development – supervision contributes to the on-going learning and maturing of the practitioner, who is constantly reviewing and refining her/his practice with an experienced colleague.

These and other arguments may need to be set against a persuasive array of counter-arguments, including those relating to:

- Cost – supervision constitutes a significant financial burden on either the counsellor or the organization.
- Time – the allocation of time within the working week 'takes away' from time spent with clients.
- Over-reliance on the supervisor – should the practitioner be more self-reliant and more able to evaluate their own activity?
- Loss of autonomy – attendance at supervision, especially where this is made obligatory, can be seen as eroding the independence of the counsellor.
- Poor quality supervision – this may impact detrimentally on the counsellor and her practice.

THE BENEFICIARIES OF SUPERVISION

Supervision is generally recognized as significantly contributing to both therapist development and the monitoring of client welfare, though there is on-going debate as to whether the counsellor or the client is primarily in the frame.

Supervisee or client?

Unsurprisingly, supervision has been shown to enhance supervisee growth specifically in the areas of self-awareness, skills, self-efficacy, theoretical orientation and through gaining support (Wheeler & Richards, 2007). However, there are only tentative findings that supervision has a beneficial impact for clients.

Although common sense would indicate that if good supervision makes an impression on the practitioner this will result in a notable positive change in the counselling relationship, this remains an assumption. Counsellors have reported supervision influencing their client work both positively and negatively – the most constructive link being that congruence and confidence in the supervisory relationship lead to increased congruence and confidence in the counselling alliance (Vallance, 2004).

> Genya left supervision feeling more at one, relaxed, clearer in her own mind. She had taken advantage of the opportunity to air a number of dilemmas. She had worked through a personal relationship problem which had been a source of constant distraction. She had unpicked a thorny client dynamic and gained clarity on how she was being drawn into a certain set of behaviours: she now felt able to be fully grounded with the client. Finally, she had explored an organizational conflict and identified how to address it with her manager.

Client welfare

There is plenty of evidence to support the importance of a warm, facilitative and trustworthy relationship in supervision, with an emphasis on striving for equality by both parties (Vallance, 2004; Weaks, 2002). This creates a climate where a supervisee is more likely to be open and honest and provides the supervisor with maximum visibility of the client work and therapeutic relationship, including concerns, worries and blunders. Without this in place a supervisor's view of the counselling work and possible ethical dilemmas can be extremely limited. The more focus on enabling the unique development of an ethical practitioner and the quality of the supervisory relationship, the better attended the client. Counsellors have described using supervision to monitor their counselling in a range of ways including exploring, reviewing and validating their work (Vallance, 2004).

It is worth noting that currently in the UK the supervisor's responsibility to clients is moral not legal, unlike that of supervisors in the US. Any move towards more legislative accountability may shift the stance of many supervisors whose trust in their supervisees would be more severely tested if they too could be called to account. Of course, any trend towards supervisory 'policing' may well lead to supervisees either becoming defensive and withholding aspects of their practice or potentially becoming overly reliant on their supervisor. Neither of these is in the best interests of clients. This represents an area of tension for supervisors faced with the challenge of offering a non-judgemental environment and attending to their professional obligations.

Philosophically and practically, humanistic-integrative supervision privileges therapist autonomy. It recognizes this value as the cornerstone in facilitating the growth of a reflective, competent, ethical practitioner with an ever stronger internal locus of evaluation operating with high levels of personal responsibility and integrity (Tudor & Worrall, 2004). Along similar lines, Mearns & Cooper (2005) contrast the principles of potentiality and deficiency, favouring supervision which emphasizes development of a supervisee's strengths rather than prioritizing their deficits or weaknesses.

FUNCTIONS AND TASKS IN SUPERVISION

The supervisory purposes outlined earlier in this chapter are delivered through three main functions: educative, supportive and management. Mutual engagement in the tasks set out in Table 1.1 ensures attention to the range of aspects which the activity needs to address in the various stages in its life.

Table 1.1 Supervision functions and tasks

Function	Educative	Supportive	Management
Tasks	• Facilitate learning • Lecture • Support • Collaborative investigation • Enable reflection • Problem solve • Teach • Provide information • Role model • Share resources	• Provide a safe place • Support • Contain • Affirm • Counsel • Build and maintain the relationship • Raise self-awareness • Reflect on dynamics • Identify systemic influences	• Assess competency • Monitor • Uphold ethical and professional practice • Protect • Gatekeep • Identify professional and ethical blind spots • Consult on organizational issues • Administrate • Review

Not all these activities appear in every relationship as some tasks may not correspond to the model of supervision being followed. The parties to the relationship tend to take responsibility for, and consciously or unconsciously favour, particular elements – which may at times restrict the scope of the activity (Carroll, 2004).

Education is central to supervision with the collective understanding that it is different to formal training, tending to be more facilitative of reflection and transforming experience into tangible learning. Support is an equally critical element. Life and client work can take its toll on counsellors and it becomes essential to have a safe place to deal with any emotional fallout, which otherwise may impact on practitioners and their clients. It is valuable to unpick personal responses to clients and organizations so as to inform client work. The extent to which certain components appear – say, sharing resources or focusing on the personal – depends on a range of factors including the participants' theoretical and philosophical preferences.

The management function attends to ethical and professional aspects, client welfare and counsellor fitness, whilst encouraging the development of the therapist's 'internal supervisor'. Again, different supervisory pairs may need to emphasize a particular range of tasks and every supervisor will have her or his own way of challenging supervisees on their practice, some preferring protection to policing.

The following two snippets of supervisory dialogue between therapist Ange and her supervisor Billy demonstrate different styles.

> **Ange:** With my client yesterday I decided to extend the session by half an hour as we seemed in the middle of really significant work.
>
> **Billy:** It's questionable whether this is ethical practice. I'd prefer you to ensure this doesn't happen again.

In contrast to:

> **Billy:** Tell me more.
>
> **Ange:** Well, as you know I've been seeing this client for some time and a theme in our work has been trust. I felt I could demonstrate my commitment to our relationship and work.
>
> **Billy:** How do you feel as you talk about it?
>
> **Ange:** A little unsettled actually.
>
> (*They go on to explore her feelings and the possible consequences of her actions, facilitating Ange to reach an informed and ethical decision.*)

In the first scenario Billy leapt into policing, possibly through his anxiety or a sense of 'rightness' from his own practice. How enabling it was for Ange or helpful to the client is questionable. In the second, Billy – although aware of a possible ethical dilemma – facilitated Ange to work it out and learning ensued.

For Reflection

- Which functions of supervision are more or less appealing to you?
- In Table 1.1, tick the tasks you would expect to be part of your supervision.
- What gaps or questions are highlighted?

CONCEPTS AND MODELS

It is possible to argue that clients don't necessarily gain more or less from therapy if they understand the approach adopted by the counsellor. The supervisee should, by contrast, be to some degree aware of the shape and structure of the supervision process if s/he is to be fully engaged in it. Counsellors who embark on the journey of supervision (towards greater insight, understanding and experience) are better served by knowing the main features of the relevant map: where are the points of reference; how might they be reached and recognized; what does it mean to be 'on the right track'?

The first phase: 'Same school' supervision

An overview of the history of supervision theory and practice reveals three main stages of development. The first may be traced back to the early part of the 20th century, originating as an element of psychoanalytical training (and later, psychodynamic), alongside theoretical teaching and the trainee's own analysis. This was a mentoring relationship with an experienced practitioner in the field assisting the development of a novice therapist. The arrangement was complicated by the supervisor frequently being also the therapist's psychoanalyst – bringing a host of ethical dilemmas associated with such a dual role, not least the conflicting purpose of these relationships (Carroll, 2004).

The nature of supervision continued to evolve alongside the emerging therapy theories, with a person-centred approach first appearing in the 1950s. This was in line with 'same school' thinking, harnessing the same set of principles for supervision as for therapy. For example, key concepts emerging from psychodynamic supervision included the idea of 'parallel process' (dynamics arising in supervision which mirror those in the therapy room) and of the 'internal supervisor' (the counsellor's capacity to self-monitor and process in time within the counselling session). In the intervening years, authors from other orientations have described their own theory-linked style of supervision, including gestalt, existential, solution-focused and cognitive-behavioural approaches.

An advantage of these 'same school' approaches is that the supervisory dyad shares a counselling theory in which the practitioner has a role model in the supervisor. There are potential limitations, however, including where blind spots in the counselling theory are also present in supervision, or where the supervisor needs to step outside the theory, say, to uphold responsibility for ethical practice (Page & Wosket, 2001).

By way of examples, what follows are brief outlines of the supervisory styles of two of the major therapeutic orientations. (Note that suggestions for further reading are provided at the end of the chapter.)

1. Cognitive-behavioural supervision

The focus of cognitive-behavioural supervision has been called 'educational, interpersonal and skill-based' (Bradley & Gould, 2001). Close attention is paid to the counsellor's client work, emphasizing the elements of case conceptualization, assessment and evaluation. The supervisor is responsible for enabling the acquisition of the knowledge and skills necessary for the type of work undertaken. There is an overt goal orientation, with strategies agreed between the parties. The educative function may be resourced by such activities as supervisor demonstration, role play, or behavioural rehearsal. Sessions may include cognitive restructuring, with the supervisor using Socratic questioning to move the counsellor to new realizations about their thought processes. The accent is on jointly agreed activity, flexibility, and adaptation of the process to the developmental needs of the counsellor (Ricketts & Donohoe, 2000; Rosenberg & Ronen, 1998).

> Kay had recently been employed by the HR department of a large employer to deliver a manualized stress and anxiety reduction programme to staff clients. Her generic counsellor training hadn't given her the specific knowledge she needed to inform her in this role. She sought a supervisor with a relevant background, and the two of them set about defining goals and strategies for ⅢⅢ▶

their work together. Gareth, her supervisor, was clear about his brief and his responsibilities, which included helping her to develop self-monitoring techniques. He explained the need for 'live' examples of her practice, and they contracted to use audio-tapes of her sessions. Kay found supervision helped her focus on her skills development and extended her theoretical knowledge. Her ability to set and review goals with clients improved. She felt that her delivery of the programme was closely scrutinized and well supported.

2. Psychodynamic supervision

Contemporary psychodynamic supervision draws extensively on a rich fund of theory and practice dating back to early psychoanalytic practice. It focuses on a range of largely unconscious patterns of relating to self and others, including transference and countertransference reactions, object relations, client resistance and psychic conflict. There is a strong emphasis on the triadic relationship and on parallel process, whereby features emerging between client and therapist may be studied through the supervisory dynamic. The counsellor is expected to link practice to theory, to advance interpretations and to evaluate the impact of her interventions in the clinical work. Supervision has an overtly educational purpose, in which there should be a balance between collaborative and authoritative elements. The safe environment of supervision is designed to deepen the counsellor's understanding of their own unconscious processes so as to improve the quality of work with the client (Ladany & Bradley, 2010).

Jeannette's placement required her to undertake in-house supervision with a psychodynamic supervisor. Coming from a different theoretical background, it took her several months to adjust to what she experienced as a challenging style of interaction in these sessions. She experienced a clear power differential with her supervisor, who nonetheless supported her work in a respectful and non-judgemental way. Jeannette became much more informed about the complexities of intra-psychic processes and the role of the therapist in identifying and challenging client ego defences. She developed her ability to empathize and to apply theory and techniques to clinical situations. Her capacity to self-monitor and self-reflect increased. So too did her appreciation of a range of ethical issues, including those attendant on contracting, boundary management and therapeutic endings.

The second phase: Developmental models

The second stage in this history arose from a recognition of the limitations of employing a therapeutic theory to engender professional growth when supervision is a developmental/consultative – rather than therapeutic – activity. In response, in the 1970–80s, 'developmental models' of supervision came about based on learning theory and contending that counsellors have predictable, progressive stages of development ranging from novice to expert or 'master-craftsman' (Littrell et al., 1979; Stoltenberg & Delworth, 1987).

These models highlight the changing needs and anxieties of counsellors at different stages and are flexible enough to be supervisee-specific. Their detractors, on the other hand, point out:

- the overly prescriptive nature of the defined phases of a therapist's development – supervisees being treated more as a category than an individual (Hawkins & Shohet, 2012)
- the 'master' or 'expert' counsellor may not be an 'expert' supervisor without additional training and/or experience (Smith, 2009)
- that practitioners are inevitably restricted by the skills and experience of their supervisor
- that there is undue focus on students and the early days of practice
- that there is limited scope for supervisors and counsellors of different orientations to work together
- that the stages of development suggest 'a hierarchy of power that favours the master as the "authority"' (Smith, 2009, p. 1).

Hawkins & Shohet (2012) have more recently advanced the developmental approach by integrating four levels of practitioner development into a 'process model', in which supervisors adapt their style and approach depending on the counsellor's level of experience, competence, individual difference and theoretical orientation.

The third phase: Integrative models

In the most recent stage of development, a range of integrative models have emerged which cross the boundaries of therapeutic approach and of level. Supervision is seen as a separate and distinct activity, leading to the evolution of specific approaches integrating a range of psychological, educational, sociological and therapeutic theories. The emphasis may be on structure, on task, on relationship – or any combination of these. Table 1.2

Table 1.2 Four integrative models and approaches of supervision

Process model	Cyclical model	Generic integrative model	Integrative relational approach
Mode 1: Reflection on content of therapy session	**Contract** – Ground rules, boundaries, relationship, expectations, accountability	**Purposes**	**The supervision process involves:**
Mode 2: Strategies and interventions	**Focus** – Issues, objectives, priorities, approach, presentation	• Client welfare • Professional development of supervisee	• Recognition of the complexity of relationships and the unique, individual contexts of client, supervisee and supervisor
Mode 3: The therapy relationship	**Space** – Collaboration, investigation, affirmation, containment, challenge	**Functions**	• Exploration of different perspectives and enabling the supervisee's view of 'self' in relationship
Mode 4: The therapist's process (therapist's countertransference)		• Educative (formative) • Supportive (restorative) • Administrative (normative)	
Mode 5: The supervisory relationship (parallel process)	**Bridge** – Consolidation, client perspective, action planning, goal setting, information giving	**Roles and tasks**	• The development of the supervisee's internal supervisor
Mode 6: Supervisor's countertransference		• Monitor administrative aspects • Set up learning relationship • Teach • Evaluate • Monitor professional/ethical issues • Counsel • Consult	• Attention to the finer nuances of the relational dynamics in both the therapeutic and supervisory relationships
Mode 6a: Supervisor/client relationship	**Review** – Feedback, grounding, re-contracting, assessment, evaluation	**Management of the process:**	• Supervisor and supervisee are 'co-subjects' and 'co-researchers' in the process of seeking meaning and insight.
Mode 7: The wider context (professional and organizational) (See *Hawkins & Shohet, 2012*)	(See *Page & Wosket, 2001*)	Pre-stage – Pre-assessment **Stage 1** – Assessing **Stage 2** – Contracting **Stage 3** – Engaging in supervision **Stage 4** – Evaluating supervisee and supervisor **Stage 5** –Terminating supervisory relationship (See *Carroll, 2004*)	(See *Gilbert & Evans, 2000*)

provides an overview of four of these models and approaches, with suggestions for further reading in the work of their originators.

These integrative approaches build on the strengths of a range of theories and avoid the limitations of both single theory and developmental approaches. Supervisor and supervisee no longer need to share a therapeutic orientation, allowing supervisors to enable the advancement of therapists from different theoretical persuasions to their own. However, there is a danger of compromise or confusion in having no single underlying philosophy, as well as the possibility that the structure could override individual need.

THE HUMANISTIC-INTEGRATIVE POSITION

> Jem had completed a humanistic counselling diploma and wanted a supervisor who would allow him to expand his theoretical horizons as well as understanding his commitment to the core values and principles of his training. He needed enough freedom to develop along his own lines as well as feeling held within a clear framework of practice. He chose a supervisor with a humanistic background who stated that she combined other elements in her work. Jem had asked some detailed questions at their introductory meeting about the style of supervision he could expect.

This book takes its inspiration from the broad field of counselling and psychotherapy known as 'humanistic-integrative'. For Jem, as for many practitioners, it is important in supervision to experience an appropriate philosophical 'home' as well as having an environment in which to develop a personal style. The following pages set out the main components that comprise the humanistic-integrative approach, with due acknowledgement that every supervisor will give the term her or his own emphasis.

Humanistic practice

The humanistic perspective draws primarily on the philosophical world of existentialism and phenomenology, whilst also being influenced by other thinking which attends to the nature of human existence and consciousness. This position adopts a holistic approach, with principles and beliefs characterized by:

- personal responsibility and autonomy
- individual potential and self-actualization

- spirituality
- individual search for meaning.

Central to humanistic therapy is the quality of an egalitarian dialogue through which clients can access their innate resources to develop and make changes so as to reach a stronger and healthier sense of self. From a supervision perspective this translates as a relationship enabling the development of an insightful, competent, confident, reflective and self-directed practitioner.

There are plenty of arguments in favour of humanistic practice as well as assertions about its limitations. All of these apply to supervisory practice just as much as to therapy. Briefly summarized, they run as follows:

Table 1.3 Arguments for and against humanistic practice

Arguments in favour of humanistic practice	Arguments against humanistic practice
• Warm	• Collusive
• Focus on a real and equal relationship	• Withholding of information
• Prizing individual experience	• Unstructured
• Enabling – encourages autonomy	• Lack of attention to the task
• Non-directive	• Insufficiently challenging
• Organic	• Fails to provide sufficient control
• Supportive	• Lacking in theoretical rigour
• Inclusive	• Lacking in intentionality
• Intuitive	• Impulsive
• Holistic	• Irresponsible

The integrative component

The addition of an integrative component to the humanistic framework reflects the well-established trend in the psychotherapies away from 'schoolism' referred to earlier. The growing awareness that no theory can fit all has led to the bringing together of different influences into the practice of many counsellors and supervisors. Integration constitutes a synthesis of elements which, for the individual practitioner, is likely to be constantly evolving. It is important, though, to be able to provide a rationale for the elements of practice being combined, as in the situation described above where Jem needed to know the detail of what was on offer from his prospective supervisor.

The synthesis provided to the client or supervisee needs to be marked by cohesion. That is, there have to be consistent elements or themes which tie the experience of the work together. The cohesion may be provided by underpinning values or philosophy (say, existential or deterministic), by the characteristics of the relationship (such as egalitarian or expert–novice), by regular use of particular styles of intervention and therapeutic strategies – or a combination of these. In other words, the selecting in and selecting out of components is thought through, as opposed to being a product of random eclecticism.

The spirit of this movement is captured by writers such as Cooper & McLeod (2010, p. 12), who define what they term the 'pluralistic' position. Their approach, they state, is 'steeped in (...) humanistic, person-centred and postmodern values' but 'can embrace, as fully as possible, the whole range of effective therapeutic methods and concepts'. Two basic principles apply:

- There is no such thing as a one-fits-all approach: different styles of intervention suit different people at different times.
- Clients should get to decide conjointly with the counsellor about how the therapy will proceed.

The notion of conjoint decision-making has a clear application to the supervisory relationship. In the absence of dialogue, supervisors might be drawn into integrating aspects which appeal to them personally and dis-counting others, regardless of the individual supervisee's needs. Conflicts could arise in situations such as where a supervisee who works well with structures and models experiences discomfort with a supervisor using a more free-flowing approach. The kinds of joint agreements being advocated by Cooper & McLeod are aimed at helping to establish what approach or style of supervisory intervention is likely to be effective and appropriate at a given time and in a given situation.

Humility and open-mindedness is called for. It helps when supervisors are clear about what is and what is not on offer in their supervision practice so as to allow for genuine supervisee choice. This clarity supports counsel-lors to develop their practice in ways which they may only be beginning to appreciate. It is wise for therapists to be curious and to inquire into their supervisor's stance on pluralism and her or his attitudes to the ever-growing multiplicity of therapy and supervision approaches available.

> In a recent supervisory review Kimmo's supervisor (Maggie) of over five years had asked him if he felt there was anything missing in their work together, explaining that in the continual develop-ment of his practice he may have emerging needs that possibly ⫸

> were not being met in their relationship. In stressing that she would welcome the opportunity to continue to work with Kimmo and adapting to meet his changing needs, Maggie also wanted to encourage him to explore the possibilities of an alternative arrangement. She recognized that he may outgrow their relationship at some point. Although Kimmo felt sure he wanted to continue working with Maggie, he also felt empowered to consider the boundaries of their work, to look out for when or if these became limitations, and to be open to different possibilities.

A flexible supervisory approach allows for the needs of counsellors to be met whose practice integrates a range of elements from the ever-growing mass of theory and research. Humanistic-integrative supervisors are well placed to facilitate the unique development of practitioners, honouring the values of self-responsibility and autonomous choice whilst not being limited by the downsides of a particular theoretical approach. For example, a humanistic-integrative supervisor may work with the concept of transference without buying into the deterministic philosophy underpinning psychodynamic theory.

Humanistic-integrative supervision

The values and principles underpinning the humanistic therapies are the thread which colours and ties together the components of humanistic-integrative supervision. Transposed from the therapeutic space, the familiar qualities reappear: empathy, acceptance, warmth, genuineness, positive regard. The supervisee's unique needs are brought to the supervision room to be explored in a way which respects the individuality of the therapeutic dyad. Our own (the authors') supervisory practice combines elements which don't necessarily appear in all humanistic settings, but which each of us have developed in different ways into our personal style:

1. attention to the unconscious elements of the relationship
2. mindfulness of the whole person of the supervisor and supervisee – including the role of physical responses, the interaction of physical and mental health, somatization and touch
3. conceptualizing the person as living in relationships and in systems (including the system of the supervisory pairing)
4. attention to transpersonal elements in the relationship
5. being open-minded about the potential for the supervisee to gain from supervisory strategies from other approaches

6. a neo-developmental element which recognizes the major shifts over time in what supervisees require from supervision – especially in the first few years of practice.

It is important for us as supervisors to remain curious – about the content of what is brought to supervision, about the supervisory relationship, about how the supervisee's needs change and evolve, and about what useful resources lie outside the usual boundaries of humanistic practice.

A key factor, explored in some detail in Chapters 4 and 9, is the integrating component of ethical and professional codes. The reference point of such a code or framework provides the indispensable container within which safe practice can be both seen and experienced to be conducted.

Implications for the supervisee

The application of integrative constructs has the potential to fuel both compatibility and friction in the supervisory relationship. At some points in our career, it is enough to know our supervisor operates from a particular stance, hoping they will adapt their style to meet our individual needs. At certain stages of our own philosophical development we may start to consider the impact of underlying similarities and differences in our supervisory relationship. Then supervisor and supervisee matching can become complex. If the two members of the supervisory dyad are from different theoretical fields or their ways of working have significantly diverged, it may be necessary to redefine where there is common ground. Even with a shared humanistic base there can still be disparate perspectives, so that exploration of broad philosophical underpinnings can be beneficial. At times like this, considerations for a counsellor include:

- avoiding assumptions about a supervisor's humanistic base
- noticing the influences the supervisor works with in both their counselling and supervision practice
- deciding how important it is to be supervised by somebody with the same philosophical foundation as one's own practice.

IN SUMMARY

A variety of different theoretical strands can be identified from the relatively short history of counsellor supervision. 'Pure brand' approaches based on therapeutic orientations vie with bespoke models of supervision and with more recent integrative and pluralistic positions. For the counsellor it is as well to be aware of the range of options for supervisory practice so that informed choices can be made. At different points in the counsellor's career it may be more or less important to find a match of orientation between therapy practice and supervision: in any case, a 'fit' between the therapy offered and the supervision received needs to be present. Whereas the professional associations regard supervision as an integral part of practice, with a less enlightened employer it may still be necessary to argue the case. In the next chapter some of the implications of a diversity of practice can be seen in the considerations to be applied when it comes to the business of choosing an appropriate supervisor.

Recommended reading

Cooper, M. & McLeod, J. (2010) 'Pluralism: Towards a New Paradigm for Therapy' *Therapy Today,* 21 (9).

Palmer, S. & Woolfe, R. (eds) (2000) *Integrative and Eclectic Counselling and Psychotherapy* (London: Sage).

Totton, N. (2010) *The Problem with Humanistic Therapies* (London: Karnac Books Ltd).

Wheeler, S. & Richards, K. (2007) 'The Impact of Clinical Supervision on Counsellors and Therapists, their Practice and their Clients: A Systematic Review of the Literature' *Counselling & Psychotherapy Research,* 7 (1), 54–65.

Chapter 2

Choosing a Supervisor

INTRODUCTION

The act of choosing a supervisor holds the pleasure of anticipation as well as the anxiety associated with making an unwise choice. We hear stories of when things go wrong as well as accounts of successful alliances. Why does it matter? In theory, the counsellor can work productively in supervision with any experienced practitioner. In practice, the experience of being a supervisee varies markedly from those who report being appropriately held and challenged to those who come away feeling unsupported or de-skilled.

The relationship between supervisee and supervisor is no less delicate in its features than that between client and counsellor. The counsellor needs an allowing space into which s/he can bring dilemmas, wonderings and uncertainties just as much as successes and stories of client gains. An appropriate choice of supervisor can enhance the therapist's level of professional satisfaction and sense of purpose as well as providing the security of knowing that, whatever occurs in the counselling room, there is always a place where worries and questions can be safely taken.

Making sense of the options

Not every counsellor has a choice of supervisor, as this chapter goes on to explore. For those with the freedom to choose, it can be hard to select from the range of provision. Typically, supervisors advertise their services with a description of what they can offer. Professional journals such as *Therapy Today* or the websites or information lines of the professional associations (BACP, UKCP, BABCP) are often a good source of supply of supervisors' details. There is a glossary of these sources at the end of the book.

Karen, a recently qualified counsellor graduating from a humanistic programme, was seeking a new supervisor subsequent to her training. From the classified advertisements in her professional journal, she drew up a shortlist based on practitioners in her local area:

Box 2.1   Seeking a supervisor

West Midlands. Psychodynamic-integrative supervisor (UKCP reg'd, Metanoia trained). Over 15 years' counselling experience. Specialist interest in bereavement and young people's counselling. Published writer/researcher. Reduced rates for trainees. Contact Dovina 01664 62****.

Derby/Midlands. Experienced NHS service manager/supervisor. £45/£35 per hour. Individuals and groups. Medical settings a specialism. E-mail catacogou@hotmail.com or phone 07755 90****.

Birmingham/West Mids. Integrative supervisor (P&W Cyclical model; CBT). Primary care settings a specialism. (£45 per hour/negotiable). Supervisor since 2005. BABCP/BACP. www.jennykilworth.com.

Derbyshire (close Sheffield and motorways). Experienced counsellor/trainer/supervisor, MBACP (Accred). Humanistic–existential orientation. £40/hour (£35/trainees/ new to profession). Contact Hamish Brown 07979 45****.

Matlock. Qualified supervisor, psychotherapist/counsellor. PG Dip, MA Couns Psych, Dip Couns Sup. BPS, UKCRP, AFT, BASRT (Accred). Psychodynamic/transpersonal/ humanistic/systemic. Contact Eileen 07778 78****.

None of these 'small ads' provides more than the briefest of details, though some reveal more, and more readily, than others. Aside from the obvious practicalities – location, cost, contact details – the advertisers' specialist expertise and experience is often stated. Other factors may be equally persuasive. Karen's course carried BACP accreditation, which draws her to a BACP supervisor, especially one who has achieved personal accreditation. Her medical background could incline her to a supervisor working in those settings. It is worth noting that we are sometimes influenced by less tangible factors. A subjective impression, such as the (for Karen) mysterious reference to the P&W Cyclical model or the bewildering drift of abbreviations in the last advertisement, can contribute to the emotional logic of our decision.

A conversation with a colleague enabled Karen to verbalize her thinking. Although her first preference was to work with a female supervisor and she was concerned to keep the cost of her supervision to a minimum, she opted to phone Hamish Brown on the basis of his professional background and status. His swift and friendly response to her approach decided her to pursue this option at least as far as the trial session he offered.

HOW DO NEEDS DETERMINE CHOICE?

For those who have the luxury of choosing their supervisor, the decision can still feel daunting. A potential supervisor may already be known in some way and the choice of this person may feel like an attractive and simple solution. Supervision with someone who is familiar and trusted can harness an already positive working relationship. However, in the longer term, disadvantages may emerge. Research suggests that dual supervisory relationships can have a tendency to become overly comfortable, collusive and lack challenge, thus limiting the supervisee's developmental process (Jesper, 2010).

It can be tempting automatically to opt for the supervisor who meets immediate, practical requirements such as those relating to fee and location. However attractive this solution may seem in the beginning, initial concerns may become overshadowed over time if the supervisor is unable to meet longer-term, developmental needs.

> William is a newly qualified counsellor with two voluntary place-ments. Without a source of regular income, he is struggling to make ends meet. He is looking for a supervisor who lives locally and who is reasonably priced to keep costs to a minimum. He decides to work with Gavin who is nearby and who charges the least of all the options that he has explored. He notices that Gavin only qualified a year before himself, but financial considerations are paramount at this stage. Sometime later, William experiences a complex ethical and legal dilemma in his practice and so he seeks emergency supervision. Gavin gets flustered, and can't offer any guidance on the matter. William's anxiety is heightened; he feels unsupported and alone in his decision-making and fears that if he gets it wrong a complaint may be made against him. He begins to wonder if he should have chosen a more experienced supervisor.

It might feel easier to go with a supervisor who has been recommended. However, one counsellor's 'good' supervisor may not correspond to another person's requirements.

Tracy is an experienced counsellor who has decided to work with a supervisor from a different orientation so as to provide a new perspective to her work. Jenny has been highly recommended by a colleague. The supervisory relationship feels more distant than Tracy is used to as Jenny's approach is more didactic and focuses specifically on the client caseload. After some months of working together, Tracy experiences a personal crisis that she feels is impacting significantly on her practice. Her supervisor's response to her bringing this up is to suggest that they postpone their session rather than spending time discussing personal issues. Tracy is left confused and hurt by this apparent rejection. After deliberating and discussing the situation with Jenny, she decides to seek a supervisor more clearly attuned to her needs.

For Reflection

- Spend some time reflecting on what it is that you want from supervision. What kind of supervisor might be able to provide this in both the short and longer term?
- Ask yourself what is important to you for your supervision to be effective.
- Identify what it is you do and don't want and then create a wish list.
- Prioritize your needs by ordering them in a fashion similar to that of Maslow's hierarchy of needs (Maslow, 1943). Table 2.1 provides some examples of the type of questions you may wish to consider.

When looking at Table 2.1, it may feel like a tall order to find a supervisor who will be able to provide everything on a list of preferences. However, by carrying out this reflective process you should be able to determine what is essential, what is desirable and then perhaps side-line those aspects that are less important. Of course, establishing if a supervisor has any of these skills or attributes will be difficult until both have had the chance to meet. Many supervisors offer an initial meeting without charge to discuss ways of working, or in some cases a trial supervision session so that a more informed choice can be made. Being able to shop around can provide a better chance of making the right choice – though this needs to be done sensitively so that supervisors are not made to feel as if they are on trial. After all, supervision is not going to be 'done' to the supervisee: it's a two-way relationship that can take some time to develop.

Table 2.1 Questions to consider when identifying your supervisory requirements

1. **Practical needs** (Physiological)
- How important is…
  - Cost?
  - Location? (Close for convenience or more distant to avoid contamination and allow 'stepping back' from the work?)
  - Accessibility of premises?

2. **Practice needs** (Safety)
- Do I want a supervisor who…
  - Is known to me?
  - Has a good reputation?
  - Is a member of a particular professional body?
  - Is accredited?
  - Has the same or different orientation/ approach?
  - Has knowledge and experience of my practice setting or specific area of work?
  - Has been in practice for a certain number of years?

3. **Relationship needs** (Social)
- How important to me is the supervisor's…
  - Gender or sexuality?
  - Ethnicity, cultural or social background?
  - Communication style and way of relating?
  - Sense of humour?
  - Warmth, empathy, acceptance, respect and congruence?
- Is there a dual relationship and if so, is this likely to cause any difficulties?
- Can we relate to each other?
- Do I want to work with someone who is familiar? How might this be in the longer term?
- Could this lead to a lack of challenge or collusion?
- Do I want a collegial and collaborative approach or would I prefer a more didactic or directive approach?
- Do I want a similar or different experience to past supervision?

4. **Developmental needs** (Self-esteem/ego)
- How important to my development is the supervisor's ability to…
  - Challenge and stretch me?
  - Be energizing, stimulating or creative?
  - Be adaptable to my learning style and developmental stage?
- Would my development be enhanced…
  - If the supervisor had the same or a different counselling orientation?
  - By the supervisor having a certain style – say, facilitative, educative or task focused?
  - If the supervisor has specific knowledge, skills or experience?

5. **Creativity, growth and fulfilment needs** (Self-actualization)
- What do I need my supervisor to offer me so that I can really grow as a practitioner…
  - A space to offload, be understood and respected?
  - A supportive and restorative space?
  - Wisdom?
  - Sensitivity?
  - A safe place where I can take risks and know that I won't be punished?
  - Creativity and imagination?
- Do I need someone who…
  - Is intuitive?
  - Is non-critical and non-judgemental?
  - Has shared beliefs and values?
- Does it feel right between us?

THE INITIAL MEETING – CAN WE WORK TOGETHER?

An initial exploratory meeting with a prospective supervisor prior to contracting can be an invaluable process for both parties. It is advisable to prepare in advance by thinking about the information that needs to be shared. Some discussion around personal and professional backgrounds can help to establish whether an effective working relationship is likely to develop. Being prepared to share openly in these early stages can aid the development of strong foundations for future work together.

> Sonia counsels in a drugs addiction agency and she herself recovered from an addiction some years ago. Sonia chose not to disclose this to her supervisor when they first met as she didn't feel that her own personal background was relevant. On discovering this later, the supervisor felt that Sonia had been withholding and incongruent. The incident created confusion and tension between them.

For those entering counselling supervision for the first time, there may be questions about protocols and professional etiquette. It's important to remember that this is a two-way process and that supervisors are also making choices about who they work with.

> Bryan has arranged to meet with a potential new supervisor at 1 p.m. on a Tuesday afternoon. Bryan arrives 20 minutes early and, being eager to meet his new supervisor, he chooses not to wait until his scheduled slot and rings the doorbell. The supervisor arranges her diary with 15 minutes between appointments and so is still busy with her previous supervisee. Bryan becomes impatient when the door isn't answered and rings the bell again. He is surprised when a rather agitated woman appears, asking him abruptly what he wants.

Although this is an innocent mistake, the relationship doesn't get off to a good start. When a supervisor works from their own home, it is easy to forget that they are running their own business and are likely to have commitments either side of appointments. Most supervisors arrange their diaries so that they have additional time for note-taking and reflection. If you arrive too early or late, then this is likely to disrupt their schedule. Try to stick to the arranged time and let the supervisor know of any delays. Some other points for consideration include:

■ Establish in advance if there is a fee for this initial meeting. Although many supervisors offer this as a complimentary session, this is not always the case.

■ On arrival, check out the supervisor's seating preference. Some supervisors may have a preferred seat whereas others may want the supervisee to choose where to sit. Wait for their cue, especially if the supervisor conducts sessions in their own home.

■ Remember that this is not a one-sided interview. Go prepared with questions but be sure to allow the supervisor to ask questions and be ready to answer these openly.

For Reflection

■ Look back over the list of needs that you created when reading the previous section.
■ Draw up a list of questions for your potential supervisor.
■ Think about what the supervisor may wish to know from you. Table 2.2 offers some suggestions.

Table 2.2 Questions for consideration in the initial session

Questions the supervisee may wish to ask the supervisor	Purpose	Questions the supervisor may wish to ask the supervisee
What is your career background?	Having an overview of each other's career background can help to identify commonalities and differences.	*What is your career background?*
How long have you been practising as a counsellor/counsellor?	You may feel more confident working with a supervisor who is more experienced than yourself. It can help the supervisor to know your developmental stage so that they can adapt their approach accordingly.	*How long have you been practising as a supervisor?*
What brought you to the counselling profession?	Again, commonalities and differences here can be useful background information as well as aiding the development of an effective working relationship.	*What brought you to the counselling profession?*

⫸

Table 2.2 (*continued*)

What is your counselling orientation and philosophy?	Exploring similarities and differences can help you decide if the supervisor's approach is going to benefit your work in supervision. If you work from different counselling perspectives, the supervisor may want to think about whether this is workable for them.	*What is your counselling orientation and philosophy?*
What is your approach to supervision? What do you expect from me?	Supervisors all have their own personal style and approach. Being able to get a sense of this will help you to decide if this is going to meet your personal and professional needs. Exploring your expectations of supervision and of each other helps to establish if the supervisor's approach fits with what you hope to get from the process and if you are both likely to make a good match.	*What are your expectations? What are you hoping to get from supervision?*
Which governing body/ethical framework do you subscribe to?	Exploring any potential differences can enable you to establish if you are both able to take this forward.	*Which governing body/ethical framework do you subscribe to?*
Are there any aspects of your personal background and current circumstances that I need to know about?	Gaining a sense of the person, getting to know each other and forming a relationship. This may also include an exploration of values and beliefs to establish if there are any commonalities or differences in this respect. Identifying any areas that might get in the way.	*Are there any aspects of your personal background and current circumstances that I need to know about?*
Where else do you/ have you worked?	Gaining a sense of the range of counselling practice and experience. Identifying any overlaps or dual relationships that may cause potential difficulties in the future and how difficulties will be addressed if they arise.	*Where do you practise? Where else have you worked?*
Do you have any specialist areas of expertise?	Do you have any shared areas of interest? Can you work together if the supervisor doesn't have experience in your specialist area? Exploring the impact of the work can inform the supervisor of how they can best support you. Some supervisors may have particular areas of work that they don't feel comfortable working with.	*What sort of counselling will you be offering? What is this like? How does this affect you?*
What days do you practise/what is your availability?	Establishing if an arrangement is practical for both.	*Does my availability suit you?*
What is your fee?	Checking if the fee is within your budget. Clarity about who will pay and how. Will the employer pay? Is there likely to be a three-way agreement?	*Who will pay me for the supervision that you receive?*

CONTRACTING

Once a counsellor and supervisor decide to start working together, the next phase involves contracting. This term, as in counselling, is used rather loosely to describe the creation of a working agreement. This is not a legally binding document, but rather a set of ground rules that outlines obligations and responsibilities, as well as some of the more practical aspects.

The process itself may be undertaken verbally or in writing, and there are no rules for how long it should take: in some cases it is brief and uncomplicated; in others it needs several sessions for an agreement to be established. Supervisors will inevitably bring their own preferences to this stage, influenced by their personal style, priorities and theoretical orientation. They may have adopted a flexible and collaborative approach, inviting the counsellor to participate in drawing up the agreement. Others are more directive, having already decided on the content of the contract, and presenting the supervisee with a written document without explicit opportunities for negotiation. The supervisor's approach at this point provides useful information about where the power is likely to sit in the evolving relationship. In our view, supervision is most effective when it is a collaborative process with, as far as possible, an equal balance of power. For some counsellors, it may feel easier in the beginning to defer to a new supervisor, seeking their lead. However, it is worth bearing in mind that this may set the tone for the longer term.

The contracting phase is an opportunity to establish the principles of the relationship as well as ensuring that some of the practical aspects are articulated. If covered with sufficient attention to detail, it is likely to pre-empt potential future difficulties and misunderstandings (Page & Wosket, 2001).

For Reflection

Before contracting, take some time to consider the following list and then identify those areas on which you would like clarification or discussion. Since each supervision dyad has its individual characteristics, only some of the following will apply.

Practical considerations:
- Frequency and duration of sessions
- Location of sessions
- The supervisor's preferred contact details; work/mobile telephone numbers, e-mail address
- Cost of sessions and how payments will be made/who will be invoiced
- Cancellations and missed sessions: What are the supervisor's expectations? Will there be a fee?   ⯈

■ Does the supervisor expect to be paid for any additional work outside the supervision space, such as providing references or writing reports for accreditation purposes?

■ How will any breaks in practice or endings be managed?

Emergency supervision:
■ Is this on offer?
■ How will you make arrangements for this?
■ Will this take place in person or over the telephone?
■ Is there an additional fee?
■ What if the supervisor is away on leave?

Roles and responsibilities:
■ Which roles and responsibilities are the supervisor's and which are the supervisee's?
■ How does the supervisor expect you to prepare for sessions?
■ Will you be required to bring any written material or audio recorded casework to supervision?
■ Will opportunities to review the supervision process be built into the process and if so, how often will these occur and in what format?

Keeping records:
■ Will your supervisor take notes during supervision and if so, what are these for? How will they be stored and for how long?
■ Is it OK for you to take notes during the session?
■ Will supervision sessions be audio recorded? If so, for what purpose?

Ethical considerations:
■ The ethical framework within which you will both work in supervision
■ How confidential is the material that you share in supervision? In what circumstances will your supervisor break confidentiality and to whom?
■ Will there be any communication with third parties? If so, why, when and how will this take place? (Examples are reports required by the training organization or feedback to the counselling agency.)
■ What action will either party take if there are concerns about the supervisee's fitness to practise?
■ What are the boundaries of your relationship? How will you manage meeting in other contexts?

Where supervision is provided in-house, the contract may be produced by the organization and be non-negotiable. Supervisor and supervisee may still profitably spend time discussing individual expectations. If counsellors are in training, a tripartite agreement between the supervisor, the training organization and the placement provider may stipulate that all parties are expected to provide feedback at certain stages. Open channels of communication such as this are necessary so as to support the trainee's developmental process. Transparency about what information is likely to be shared, with whom, when and how, will help to put the supervisee and supervisor at their ease.

EXPECTATIONS OF THE SUPERVISION SPACE

Ask any group of counsellors what they expect supervision to be like and you'll get a range of responses coloured by individual experience. A positive previous relationship with a mentor or tutor might lead to expectations of an empathic and allowing space. Memories of an unsatisfactory experience could fuel anticipation of having to be compliant or reassuring towards the supervisor.

Leaving aside the influence of personal history, there are likely to be common themes:

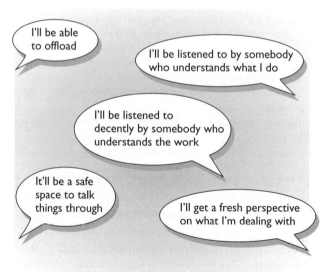

It is reasonable to anticipate that supervision will provide a sounding board, a place where questions and dilemmas can be safely aired and explored. The fundamental hope is for a meeting of professionals with the common purpose of enhancing and extending competence in the service of the client.

The elements of such a relationship have a much more subjective quality than the practical aspects discussed earlier. How can the supervisee gauge these less definable attributes of the supervision space in the initial stages so as to evaluate actual experience against expectations? The key is to be open to one's own responses on an affective as well as a cognitive level. Do you feel safe with this person? Do you feel clear about or a little confused by what the supervisor has to say? Does s/he seem to be ethically aware? Can you imagine feeling psychologically held once established in this relationship? Will boundaries be respected? Will you feel understood when things aren't going so well? Will the supervisor offer support without being prescriptive – leaving you to make your own judgements about practice?

The responses to these and similar questions are necessarily based on a whole range of personal impressions, but demand sufficient scrutiny on the part of the supervisee in the early stages in order for trust in the person and the process to unfold. Too much uncertainty around issues of psychological safety may hinder the development of a helpful relationship.

As with the practical questions outlined above, it is for the supervisee to determine those areas on which clarification is needed. The initial meetings should, as a minimum, enable the counsellor to get a sense of the potential of this relationship and the degree to which questions and uncertainties can be safely aired.

Many beliefs which install themselves early on relate to what the supervisee imagines to be the supervisor's expectations of *them*. These could range from not being seen to have made a mistake, or needing to have read up on every client issue that emerges, or never showing vulnerability. The supervisee may imagine that s/he can only present successful or complete pieces of practice, or else is not supposed to challenge the supervisor's views, perception or behaviour.

However clear the focus on these and similar aspects at the outset, there is no denying that experience can bring a different view, as both Katie and Sam discovered:

> Katie, a first year trainee beginning her placement, opted to work with John as her external supervisor. He was polite and had an academic background that matched her own. However, he forgot ⇒

to attend for their second supervision session and his apologies seemed to lack conviction. In subsequent sessions, it was clear that he lacked experience and seemed somewhat preoccupied. Katie maintained the arrangement but felt annoyed with herself for what she saw as 'going through the motions'.

Sam was hoping that her first experience of supervision would support her steep learning curve in her new job in an Occupational Health unit. However, she soon realized that Donna, her supervisor and manager, had not had any counselling training and wasn't familiar with discussions about the complex dynamics with which she was grappling in client work. She also became concerned about her manager's stress levels. Their meetings seemed to be dominated by Donna's offloading her troubles.

In reality, it is only by checking over time the validity of one's early judgements that these can be properly tested. In the two examples below, Jack and Jessica felt themselves constrained to explore the robustness of the arrangement. To their credit, they had the courage to raise the issue troubling them – and to the supervisor's credit, the response was sensitive and appropriate. There is no way of knowing how the supervisor will respond – but a clear and self-aware approach to difficult moments such as these can lead to a strengthening of the emerging bond between the two parties.

Jack found himself mired in a string of health-related problems. Shortly after beginning his supervision arrangement, he had exploratory surgery which revealed complications needing further intervention. Aside from anxieties about these procedures, Jack worried about how his absence from work and a period of incapacity would impact on his competence. He was anxious that his supervisor would judge him unfit to practise. He decided to share his concerns fully with his supervisor, and was pleasantly surprised to find that a highly constructive session ensued, helping him to plan strategies for different eventualities.

Jessica hadn't been working long with her supervisor. She left one supervision session feeling troubled but not knowing why. The more she considered it, the more she felt judged and misunderstood by the supervisor. She had not really needed to challenge her supervisor before and wasn't convinced she had the right to do so. She took the risk of raising her experience at the beginning of their next meeting – not in a blaming way, and taking responsibility for her own input. The supervisor's response was open and non-defensive. As a result of this incident, their relationship was strengthened.

Whilst gospels of perfection are unlikely to be useful guides – what supervisor can match some imagined ideal? – it is still appropriate to expect to work with a supervisor who is interested in your work, and who is concerned for your welfare and that of your clients. The effort, time and money which are expended in accessing supervision mean that it is reasonable to expect professional and ethical integrity, open dialogue, an ability to challenge and (as in the example above) to be challenged themselves.

WHEN THE CHOICE OF SUPERVISOR IS LIMITED

For many counsellors, the freedom of unrestricted choice of a supervisor does not apply. Those in training or working in organizations requiring in-house supervision frequently experience a different set of challenges when it comes to establishing a relationship with a new supervisor.

Trainees typically face the necessity of choosing from a list of supervisors drawn up by the training organization. From the point of view of the organization, the approved list offers a degree of standardization and a guarantee of communication concerning the welfare and progress of the student counsellor. From the trainee's perspective, any supervisor who has been accepted onto the list should, at least in theory, correspond to the norms of the training programme and be aware of the usual processes and procedures – for example where an end-of-year statement or report is required. The supervisor's approach to supervision should also meet the requirements of the tutor team, whether or not their therapeutic orientation matches that of the course.

Institutions vary between those who allocate students to a supervisor, and those who offer unrestricted choice from an approved list. The choice of a first supervisor can feel onerous for the student. It is worth reiterating that no two supervision dyads are ever quite alike: one trainee's perfect match could feel an uneasy fit for another person.

For the trainee entering into this kind of 'tied' agreement, it is essential to know the nature of the strings attached to the arrangement. In the initial meeting, it's advisable to clarify the role the supervisor will play in assessing and reporting on you, the trainee. Will you have any input in communications with the tutors? How collaborative is the process of writing reports? What are the mechanisms for dialogue with the tutors or with the placement agency, should that ever be required? Many training institutions set out the nature of these processes in their documentation – so the student may be fortunate in having these questions answered in advance.

On the plus side, working with a locally approved supervisor usually means that:

- they are known to the institution and the standard of their work should be reliable
- they are tied in to the organization's procedures and communication channels
- they should be knowledgeable about the course and offer an approach which dovetails with the orientation of the training
- (not least) they may well offer a reduced student rate.

On the other side of the balance sheet:

- it may be difficult to change supervisors even if the relationship does not develop harmoniously
- trainees may feel inhibited, fearing that use of the supervision space is being judged and reported on, perhaps negatively
- the selection on offer doesn't correspond to individual needs – which may quite simply mean lack of a supervisor close to home.

Most arrangements in training work out well or well enough to complement learning on the course. Sometimes, though, there are difficult conversations to be had with tutors and with a supervisor whose approach just doesn't support one's style of learning. Generally, it is least problematic (or embarrassing) to make a change at the end of an academic year, so 'hanging on in' and gaining experience in the meantime can be the best strategy. The processes involved in changing a supervisor can provide significant learning in themselves, despite – or perhaps because of – the discomfort which may be involved.

Agency-based supervision

Agency-based supervision, which may be a condition of employment, can also have potentially advantageous and – at times – problematic elements. There are obvious practical benefits in having free, local support from a person who understands the environment and client population. It may be, though, that there are difficult power dynamics to negotiate, as in cases where managerial supervision seems to require a recitation of casework details rather than in-depth exploration, or where the counsellor feels the need to comply with the manager's views or accede unquestioningly to organizational priorities.

Practical barriers to choice

Other life situations which restrict choice have their origins in physical or psychological settings. Counsellors who work in remote locations with no access to a supervisor within reach may choose to access supervision by telephone, a skype link or online. Physically disabled counsellors may also find it useful to employ electronic technology (e-mail, MSN) to support their supervision. Chapter 8 explores the potential of some of these more recent forms of practice.

Responses to enforced or restricted choice

It can be reassuring that the anxiety of choice is removed or reduced in the situations just described. In agency or training contexts, someone else has taken the responsibility and made the effort to locate you a supervisor. Quality assurance is at least in part assumed by the organization. Where external circumstances confine the choice, the arrangement arrived at can feel containing rather than restricting.

Where the sense of constraint prevails, it is worth attempting to:

- approach the contracting stage with as much clarity as possible about your perceived needs
- be patient and realistic about the development of the relationship, and taking concerns about the dynamic and process respectfully back to the supervisor
- learn to appreciate what *this* supervisor can offer from her or his professional perspective and experience
- use peer support to explore issues which cannot be constructively explored in the formal supervision arrangement.

EARLY DAYS

> Tim was surprised how anxious he was in his first few supervision sessions. Although he could recognize that his new supervisor, Judy, had done her best in the trial session to put him at his ease, he felt distinctly out of his comfort zone. Entering the world of counselling at age 50 after a career in business, he was reminded in these sessions of arriving at a new school and not knowing the rules. He was having problems establishing a client base and felt he was failing every time a client didn't turn up for a session. Having to 'confess' this to Judy made him feel like a 12-year-old boy again, owning up to the teacher for not having done his homework.

The first few sessions in supervision may well be influenced by all manner of long-buried memories or cognate experience. Other contexts in which the supervisee is in the one-down position may re-surface and the emotions prompted can be unwelcome companions in this new relationship. For others, positive experience in a previous relationship may intrude rather too often, obscuring the awareness of the here-and-now. A counsellor may be missing the style and approach of a previous supervisor more than s/he recognizes and feeling resentful and dissatisfied that the new person doesn't come up to scratch. Until this has been brought into awareness, it is difficult to fully commit to the new relationship and to discover the full range of what it can offer.

Aside from sometimes troublesome influences from the past, there is all the newness of the present to deal with. Supervisees have to learn the style of their supervisor, and how to make use of the framework on offer. The structure may seem more or less formal or formulaic, the approach more or less in keeping with the counsellor's own way of working with clients.

The supervision space may well be one where the supervisee learns to appreciate (or to appreciate more profoundly) the culture of counselling. By 'culture' is meant the norms and standards, vocabulary, and ways of doing and being which have come to characterize the different strands within the profession. For the new practitioner especially, the challenges of learning to marry their personal style with the conventions of the therapeutic approach can be discomforting at times.

> A part of Tim's learning lay in the area of directiveness. His supervisor's style of facilitation demonstrated to him that his managerial approach could be a hindrance in the therapy room. The sessions challenged him to adopt a different style from the one which had served him well in his previous role.

HINTS AND POINTERS

The initial stages of any supervision relationship can feel like uncharted territory, with all the feelings that accompany the start of an unfamiliar journey. The following pointers may be usefully borne in mind in these early days.

1. **Respect your own experience.** The resources which supervisees bring in from previous personal and professional experience can prove of incalculable value in the therapy room. Whilst supervision may be a

space in which the counsellor is learning to grow into a new role and identity, it is not a given that previously acquired competences, understandings or ways of being must be universally abandoned. Better to be judicious in harnessing existing capacities and experience in the service of the client.

2. **Supervision can feel as unfamiliar to the supervisee as does therapy to the new client.** The anxieties and uncertainty which sometimes emerge in supervision may provide experiential understanding of how it is for new clients, for whom the therapeutic relationship feels unknown – calling into question as it does all sorts of basic assumptions out of which they operate in other contexts in their lives.

3. **Active collaboration works better than a pattern of compliance.** Though supervisees may be less knowledgeable and experienced than the supervisor, it can be unhelpful for this position to inform the relationship too strongly. Better for the counsellor to remind themselves of the strengths they naturally bring to other personal and professional relationships – situations in which they have shown themselves to be effective and authoritative.

4. **Try out what works.** Experimentation with a range of behaviours can enhance the value of supervision. These could include jotting down key points in the session, noting references the supervisor offers, allocating time to debrief the session in a quiet place, or ensuring supervision isn't crammed into a busy day so that there is little time or energy for reflection before or following the session.

5. **Framework the session** by letting the supervisor know what is going on in the broader canvas of your life. Not all supervisors are open to this, yet there are good arguments for account to be taken of contextualizing experience, especially where this is having a significant impact on the counsellor.

6. **Learn to be tolerant, understanding and accepting of yourself in supervision** – warts and all – just as you would hope to be towards clients in the therapy room. A classic case of 'do to yourself as you try to do to others'.

7. **Use the time available.** If you have 10 minutes left at the end of the session, this is long enough to sketch the bare bones of an issue and pose a question to which both supervisor and supervisee have time for an initial response.

8. **Supervision isn't a performance.** If it seems as if it is, ask yourself what that means about how you are presenting and what you are seeking to achieve.

9. **Confidence and trust build slowly.** These are unlikely to be components of the supervision relationship at the outset. Putting down the sorts of markers which foster these elements is likely to bear fruit in the longer term: honesty, clarity, tolerance, sensitivity to the other person, the stage of the relationship and the process – plus a measure of preparedness to say it how it is.

10. **Respect your own values.** It is the supervisee's personal philosophy which has brought them into the profession and is the foundation of the therapeutic relationship they seek to build. Since identity and values are closely allied, it is likely that developments in the counsellor's professional identity may well prompt reflections on values and beliefs. A supportive supervision space can foster such reflections and pave the way for new insights.

IN SUMMARY

Any number of factors may be significant in informing the therapist's choice of supervisor. It is worthwhile not just to take a proactive stance to reviewing the available options, but also to reflect on how our developmental needs may change over time. At an initial meeting, how much does the counsellor need to share with the prospective supervisor, and what details are required from them to inform the decision? Trainees – and many agency workers – may have specific factors to consider, and need clarity about communication channels and the division of responsibility. In the end, it may be the less tangible elements which are influential in deciding whether to proceed.

Once the arrangement is established, there may still be difficult moments to negotiate. How problems are aired and resolved can influence the future quality of the supervision experience. It is in any case reasonable to expect the early days with a new supervisor to bring challenges on both sides. Most reliably, the counsellor can expect to derive benefit from supervision when s/he brings to the meetings a mix of pragmatism, self-respect, tolerance and a willingness to allow the gradual development of a collaborative relationship.

Recommended reading

Despenser, S. (2011) 'What is Supervision?' *BACP Information Sheet (S2)* (Lutterworth: BACP).

Inskipp, F. & Proctor, B. (2009) *Making the Most of Supervision*, 2nd edn (Twickenham: Cascade).

Jacobs, M. (1996) *In Search of Supervision* (Buckingham: Open University Press).

Walker, M. & Jacobs, M. (2004) *Supervision Questions and Answers for Counsellors and Therapists* (London: Whurr).

Chapter 3

How to be a Supervisee

INTRODUCTION

There is a common assumption that counsellors know how to engage with the complex, intensive and interactive process of supervision. Whereas supervisory activity partly mirrors that of the therapeutic process, it has its own character, the details of which may well seem undefined at the outset. This chapter sets out the elements of the process to enable the counsellor to prepare and use the sessions to gain the many benefits on offer.

PERSONAL CHALLENGES

Each person has their particular style of engagement and depth of contact in their various relationships. A supervisee's level of connectedness with self and others will influence the meaningfulness of their relationships with both clients and supervisor. It is an on-going challenge to continue to develop self-awareness and interpersonal skills whilst managing the pressures of client and service needs. A counsellor who works towards increasing self-knowledge and self-acceptance is likely to find that this enhances their ability to be congruent and trusting of their own reactions, which in turn influences the depth and complexity of their relationships with others. Supervisees who are more aware of their thoughts and emotional responses have a resource for making progress in their level of rapport. This contributes to creating the optimum climate for personal and professional growth. Questions such as 'What am I feeling now?' and 'What is going on between us?' bring a here-and-now mindfulness which can highlight elements in the supervisory relationship just as effectively as in the relationship with the client. Determination may be needed to address issues that arise from this heightened awareness.

The following is an example of intrapersonal and interpersonal awareness and demonstrates that when a supervisee is struggling, feeling embarrassed or ashamed, it can take considerable resolve to be congruent. However, the benefits of adopting that position can be significant.

> *Giorgio managed to overcome his reticence to tell his supervisor, Huw, that he had disclosed personal information to his client. He looked distressed as he spoke.*
>
> **H**: Say more about your reasons for that disclosure.
>
> **G**: I was trying to tell him it was OK to feel like that. Now I am ashamed that I took over his space with my stuff.
>
> **H**: What was his reaction?
>
> **G**: His face relaxed and he then talked more openly about his experience of abuse and shared things that he had kept hidden up to now.

After taking the risk to disclose his 'error' and embarrassment, Giorgio was facilitated to reach a more balanced view of his intervention. This led to further reflection and enabled learning about therapist disclosure and relationship dynamics.

It is important for supervisees to use this kind of opportunity to address their own feelings and concerns and to take responsibility for self-development. The risk if this does not occur is that it can eventually stifle the capacity for reflexivity and prevent access to the wisdom that client work demands.

For Reflection

Consider the level of your engagement in supervision:

- If you feel less engaged in some or many of the sessions:
  - What affects that?
  - What gets left out?
- What action could you take to adjust your engagement in supervision?

BOUNDARY BETWEEN SUPERVISION AND PERSONAL THERAPY

It is a commonly held notion that supervision is entirely distinct from therapy. In our view the idea that there is a clear line of demarcation between these two activities is inaccurate. The challenge for each supervisory pair is to 'draw their line' and to be able to determine when and if supervision falls into therapy. In situations where this occurs, it is likely that the visibility of client and practice is lost. Areas of overlap and differences between the two activities are outlined below:

Table 3.1 Drawing the line between supervision and counselling

Potential areas of overlap between counselling and supervision	Where supervision differs from counselling
• Development of self-awareness • Personal development • Gaining support • Self-care, monitoring and attending to the well-being of the counsellor • Sharing personal difficulties and dilemmas	• Debating ethical, moral and legal dilemmas • Exploring and attending to client conceptualization, process and welfare • Unpicking client–counsellor dynamics • Examining how therapeutic theory applies to practice • Working through organizational challenges and conflicts • Developing professional skills • Attending to and monitoring continuing professional development • Developing one's own approach • Debating trends in the profession

Historical issues

Through discussing a counselling relationship a practitioner can reawaken past personal events which, when explored in supervision, can develop self-awareness and benefit their practice.

> **Nina** (*supervisor*): Tell me more about how you feel when you are with this client?
>
> **Otto**: I feel her sadness, but to be honest I also feel frustrated.
>
> **Nina**: You sound frustrated now.
>
> **Otto**: Frustrated at her reluctance to help herself… to make any change.
>
> ⫸

> **Nina**:You're experiencing her sadness and the frustration is your own at her lack of change.
>
> **Otto**:You're right, my frustration… it's reminding me of years ago when I was bullied and I did nothing at all to help myself. I was really terrified and angry too. I just let it happen, let it go on.
>
> (*Otto talks at length about this episode in his life and the feelings he still has about it.*)
>
> **Otto**: I hadn't realized how angry I still am about that time.
>
> **Nina**:And something about your client has accessed that anger.
>
> **Otto**:Yeah and it's misplaced. It's muddying the water with this client. I'm no longer feeling it. Now I know what it's about and know to leave it… My job is to assist this client to understand how she is feeling about her situation and work out what she wants to do about it.

Significantly here, although personal material was delved into, the insight was brought back and applied to the client work.

Current stresses

A level of unburdening and attendance to the well-being and the self-care of the supervisee is a necessary function of supervision, ensuring optimum capability and fitness to practise. The withholding of any reference to personal stressors can be detrimental to the process as a supervisor might sense something is awry, but be unable to aid their supervisee with it. Listening to and empathizing with clients' stories and emotions can take its toll. Therapists can be affected in a number of ways, from feeling worn down and burdened to being shocked or traumatized. The actual impact can be hidden until exploration in supervision identifies the root of, say, the counsellor's sense of generalized apathy. The discussion may act as a wake-up call, providing insight and enabling the counsellor to monitor herself more effectively. (Note that Chapter 9 deals further with the significance of self-care.)

Counsellors do carry personal material into their client relationships which, if unexamined, has the potential to contaminate the therapeutic work. By addressing personal situations in supervision, feelings can be acknowledged, potential influence on practice can be assessed and plans made. Where a counsellor is facing a stressful personal situation there is a balance to be struck in supervision between allowing a potentially destabilizing experience to take over sessions and attending directly to professional practice. Ideally a supervisory pair will decide together which elements to cover in supervision and what would be better addressed elsewhere.

> Peter's father is terminally ill. He is feeling distressed and anxious. With his supervisor he acknowledged that he would need time off work and possibly counselling. He talked to his organization and lined up further support. Throughout the months of his dad's decline time was spent in supervision reviewing the situation, but both parties were able to ensure that his clients and practice were also attended to, holding a focus on his fitness to practise and self-care. It would have been concerning if Peter had kept this on-going personal situation from the supervisory space, his supervisor perhaps detecting all was not well, inhibited from assisting and maybe feeling distanced. This in turn could have been an indicator of a similar distance emerging in Peter's therapeutic relationships.

Catching a drift

Although counsellors need a safe place where their struggles can be disclosed, supervisees must not lose sight of the goals and boundaries of supervision. It is important to keep in mind the question 'How is this dialogue going to influence my practice?' Without doubt there are times when supervision feels like therapy, so it makes sense to be able to evaluate what is and is not appropriate. Indicators that a drift has occurred or is occurring include:

Box 3.1 Indicators that the balance between supervisory functions needs adjustment

- Little attention to clients over a series of sessions
- Repeated examination of the counsellor's personal history and current stresses
- Lack of linking between personal exploration and counselling practice
- Fronting up with personal material as a way of avoiding talking about client work
- No observable insight or behavioural change on the part of the counsellor

---

PREPARING FOR SUPERVISION

The level of supervisory engagement and quality of outcomes can be enhanced by careful preparation. Every counsellor has their preferred way of identifying topics for supervision. It is possible, though, to fall into repetitive ways of preparing for supervision which, although fruitful, can become limiting. Whilst a lack of formal preparation can bring spontaneity and creativity to the session, it may deny the opportunity to examine more deeply the therapeutic relationship. On the other hand, over-preparation can be stultifying, holding a supervisee in a familiar and safe pattern and impeding exploration. If your preparation becomes routine then trying out different and creative ways of presenting in supervision can give new energy and interest.

Options for preparation

In the run-up to a session, there is probably no end to the range of topics which could emerge as potentially productive to bring to supervision. The following are pointers to the diversity of that range, which every counsellor will develop to suit their own needs.

1. Specific areas for reflection

- What is going on for you with respect to a specific client, their story or behaviours?
- Client material, behaviours or emotions generating raised anxiety or preoccupation in you, such as self-harm, suicidal thoughts, risky behaviour, extreme low mood, delusional thinking, or uncontrollable anger.
- What has worked well and what has not?
- The context of your client's life and the location in which they are seen.
- The counselling process: where is your client in their story?
- Processes identified – such as 'stuckness' in either person, transference or countertransference.
- Relationship quality and possible collusion.

2. General areas for reflection

- Too many or too few clients – since both situations have implications for practice and may require action.
- Wonderings, specific questions, dilemmas, ethical issues, boundaries, professional relationships or organizational aspects.
- Noticing what is brought regularly to supervision and what is normally left out.

Different options

The opportunities offered by the supervision space relate both to what is brought as material for reflection and to the style of presentation.

In terms of content, the context in which the therapy is offered may be as demanding of attention as is the client work itself. Issues of organizational change, staff dynamics and the management of protocols can be a dominant feature in the practitioner's working day. It may be relevant and important to discuss broader professional developments and their impact on counsellor and clients.

As to the activity in the therapy room itself, it can be useful for the counsellor to focus in supervision on recurrent themes in their own behaviour. These could range from the tendency to talk too much or intervene too little; to ask too many questions, give advice or problem solve. It may be that the counsellor has noticed a reluctance to challenge, or difficulty with managing endings. Feelings or thoughts which emerge with clients could also be the focus – being angry at the system, lacking enthusiasm, feeling anxious. Sometimes it can seem as if we are 'carrying something' just out of awareness: talking this through can catch previously unregistered aspects of the client and the therapeutic relationship.

Relationship challenges in a supervisee's professional or personal life may need to figure from time to time so that supervision can help explore how these are impacting on counselling relationships.

It can be beneficial to change presentation patterns for supervision sessions. The use of metaphor, narratives or creative methods – colour and paper, images or shapes to depict client patterns, relationship dynamics or specific questions – can highlight previously unseen elements as well as clarifying struggles and successes.

The presentation of a tape recording of the therapy session can assist in identifying concerns by bringing the live interaction into the room. Dynamics, skills and the quality of presence of the therapist are all evident. To ensure efficient use of time and to get what is needed from the process it is important to choose a part of the taped session and to request discussion and feedback on specific areas.

Preparing for managing time

Deliberation given to the level and intensity of the caseload can assist in prioritizing the time allocation for each client and in identifying which ones can be held over for another session.

Supervisees with short-term clients or a heavy caseload may tend to require more factual and practical outcomes. Those working with long-term clients or with high intensity material may need to allow for a fuller description of the client, their problems and a longer restorative phase in the supervision process.

Recording supervision

Session taping or note-taking needs to be mutually agreed. Both parties should be aware of the rationale for the recording, and agree on confidentiality, storage systems and the duration of the arrangement. In some situations notes are needed to meet ethical, legal or organizational requirements, as where an employer requests a brief account of topics taken to supervision.

Trainee supervisees may wish to tape sessions to aid coursework preparation, so as to include detailed information when writing up client notes and supervisory discussions. For others, the need to take notes will be prompted by their individual learning style or to assist memory. Some take quick notes of key points as the session progresses; others like to stop the session to write verbatim the supervisor's words. Supervisors could have concerns about the last method if it begins to indicate an inability to think for oneself.

For Reflection

- What is your preparation process for supervision?
- To what extent does this assist you in getting your needs and those of your clients met?
- What could enhance your experience of supervision and its appropriateness to your client work?

DIFFERENCE

A bewildering range of factors contribute to the individuality of client and counsellor, from ethnicity to language, physical presentation to social class, age and gender to life experience. Add to these our values and beliefs, learning styles, tastes and preferences and other less easily definable components, and the list of possible areas of distinctiveness and difference starts to look daunting.

Our world view is intrinsic to who we believe we are and how we make sense of our experiences. Our values, ways of thinking, feeling and learning will themselves be influenced by personal history and environment. At its most basic, our understanding of what it means to be human has a profound effect on how we work with clients as well as in the supervision space. One such understanding applies to the (Western) emphasis on individuality, as distinct from the conceptualization of the person first and foremost in relation to family and community.

Same culture, different constructs

> Philip used a problem management approach with his short term clients. He wanted affirmation of how he was working. Polly occasionally asked him what he felt and what dynamics were present in his client–counsellor interactions. When relating a dilemma in trying to facilitate a client moving on from telling his story, he felt unheard and was unable to answer as the question did not seem apposite. As he reflected further he thought he was being forced to contemplate an aspect that he did not consider important at this stage. He felt his supervisor was operating from her own, possibly female, constructs and ways of working rather than accepting that his client needed results.

In this example Philip expected focus and action and did not understand his supervisor's encouragement to look at the relationship dynamics. The two of them appeared to hold different frames of reference. It was important for him to raise this in his next meeting with Polly.

Gender and cultural influences

> Rana's family were second generation immigrants to the UK. Her grandparents came from the Philippines and her family had strong values about working hard, respecting elders and honouring those with higher status and learning. She chose her supervisor Michael from a list at university and felt she would be well supported as he was male, highly qualified and experienced. Rana was expecting fatherly advice. What she got was challenges to come up with her own ideas of how to work with clients. The dynamics between the two of them became tense and unhelpful to her.

In this example Michael had not understood Rana's cultural frame, and interpreted her respect and deference as lack of assertiveness and dependency. Rana's professional development required her to become more confident in her own knowledge and experiences as well as to appreciate the importance and influence of more than one set of values. This began to happen when each of them realized the importance of listening carefully to each other's value statements, and separately initiated dialogue about the beliefs underlying the tensions between them. For both people involved – but for Rana in particular – this constituted a major challenge, and one that called on her determination to succeed in this profession.

> Ishmail's parents were born in Pakistan. His parents arrived in Northern England in the late fifties. He is a counsellor in an inner city youth project where he encounters a diversity of ethnic, cultural, class and religious values. He chose his male supervisor with care following earlier episodes in supervision where he had felt unable to explore the presence of his cultural and family background as it affected his practice. As time went by, Ishmail felt his supervisor Mackenzie had little comprehension of the tensions involved in working and living with clients from closely knit families in a deprived inner city community.

Ishmail found he became defensive and angry at not being able to make himself understood. Whilst this was a useful reminder of the struggles of his clients, it was less than facilitative for him in the complexity of his work. He realized he needed to revise his assumptions about his use of supervision and face himself and Mackenzie with finding a new way of working together.

For Reflection

Think about the interactions between you and your supervisor.

■ To what extent are these interactions supportive or inhibitive to your understanding of difference in your work and in supervision?
■ If you sense any difficulties in understanding because of difference, how do you manage these?
■ Remind yourself about how you have managed yourself in similar situations in the past. Can any of those strategies be used to bring your concerns to supervision?

Working it out

Francesco worked in a voluntary service for gay, lesbian and bisexual people. The boundaries in this agency appeared flexible and adapted to client needs. His supervisor Rebecca had strong views about holding firm boundaries in therapy and supervision. They had been working together for a few months when a conflict arose as Francesco mentioned meeting and chatting to a client at a social occasion held by the centre.

R: You seemed to be drawn into talking with him.

F: Erm, erm. (*unsure how to respond*)

R: What about the need to keep a distance from your client?

F: (*irritated*) The whole 'raison d'être' of the agency is for no false separation between us. We're all human beings with similar backgrounds of discrimination and exclusion. So we don't keep apart from one another.

R: (*noticing the strength of feeling*) Now I feel embarrassed because I made a clumsy intervention. Tell me more about how you maintain boundaries.

F: Flexible boundaries do not mean there are none. We have to agree with each client how we will manage social interactions and meeting in different parts of the agency as we are all involved in other activities. We're clear about what belongs in each place and we challenge any slip or intentional attempt to break boundaries.

After this difficult interaction, Rebecca gained a clearer understanding of how Francesco worked in an agency which at first glance held boundaries loosely. This enabled him to be more open in subsequent sessions and Rebecca to value his ability to work out and manage problems in a complex working environment.

Issues of difference are by their very nature difficult to broach, and not easily understood either by a supervisee or by a supervisor struggling with such complexity in supervision. Lago (2006, p. 58) talks of the 'iceberg conception of culture' where the aspects of culture of which we are aware constitutes the one third above the water, leaving two thirds below the surface of which we are only dimly aware.

In the world outside the counselling room, more visible differences – say, due to physical impairment or characteristics such as physiognomy or skin colour – often give rise to situations experienced as oppressive. Supervision may be a forum for investigating whether the counsellor's reactions to certain clients are internal and learned or evidence a lack of awareness or are in response to others' repressive behaviours.

Managing feelings of disempowerment

Supervisees from any minority group can be challenged when finding their place in a majority culture, the counselling profession and the workplace. Standing out as different because of gender, race, class, ethnicity or culture can take its toll on the emotional and personal identity of an individual and is complex and contextual in nature. The dilemma of whether, or how much, to assimilate into the dominant culture is a struggle for some. It can lead to stress and a fragmentation or a compartmentalization of the self when identity is suppressed. It is true, of course, that many people successfully manage their relationship with the dominant culture. Some, indeed, become leaders or mentors in educating others about the importance of welcoming difference in all its forms.

It is important to take note when feelings of disempowerment related to difference emerge in supervision. Reflecting on the origins of her responses, the counsellor may conclude that the mainspring of the distress or discomfort lies in the all-round experience of living as a member of a minority group. A significant question for the supervision relationship concerns the extent to which the supervisor's interactions are contributing to the sense of being misunderstood or oppressed. The supervisor may be unaware of the impact of remarks, language or behaviours – perhaps because of a lack of relevant experience or familiarity with problems the supervisee knows to be real. It is important to retain sufficient self-belief and to access appropriate support. This may, in time, provide the counsellor with the clarity and resources she needs to take the issue back to the supervisor.

Learning styles

Learning styles play a key part in supervision as in any educative endeavour. The learning cycle of activity, assimilation, abstraction and application is not always an easy process and we each have elements we favour and parts we find difficult. We have a mix of ways of thinking and doing, rather than one specific style, but are inclined to access regularly the same one or two strategies. Some people need to think carefully first, gather facts and weigh up possibilities before coming to a conclusion and putting that into action. They prefer supervisors to listen, question and reflect back to ensure everything has been covered. Others rely more on intuition or 'gut feelings', needing the supervisor to encourage, but not to ask them to explain their reasoning.

Learning mainly through doing, reflecting afterwards and then reviewing what has happened means that our main active learning may well be outside the supervision sessions. Supervision may then be used to check out and affirm or adjust that process where appropriate.

Some individuals can of course pick out pertinent points quickly and accurately with their auditory learning ability and memory; others have a visual propensity to their learning, work well with metaphor, or need a solid theoretical understanding before interacting with their client.

Honey & Mumford (1993) built on the work of Kolb (1984) to describe four different ways of learning which are described below in relation to supervision.

For Reflection

■ Rate on a scale of 0–5 in the grid below how much of each learning style you recognize in yourself. Place a score for each style in the right-hand column to identify which is your predominant way of learning (0 = not at all; 5 = strong preference).

■ You may find that you are able to relate to elements in each learning style, but it is likely that one or two will emerge as being more dominant.

■ How could this impact on your use of supervision?

Rating 0–5

Activists   Learn through doing without knowingly engaging in analysing. Prefer a supervisor who encourages them to try things out. Mistakes are viewed as valuable learning. Risk is managed by challenges to reflect and pull out learning.   ☐

Reflectors   Like to observe and think about what happened, consider all angles before coming to a conclusion and need time to check things out thoroughly. Can get overly interested in the opinion of their supervisor and want to carefully think through possible effects of any new knowledge.
Integration of learning may not be noticeable in the supervision session and be seen at a later date.   ☐

Theorists   Learn through cognitive analysis and the application of theories. Prefer abstracting rules and generalizations and using these to guide future actions. Enjoy new theories and can get into academic debates. Risk using theory to avoid real contact with their supervisor.   ☐

Pragmatists   Learn 'practically' like an apprentice would alongside a person with more knowledge. Prefer to be given practical suggestions and solutions. May focus on whether something will work or not and can feel unsure with a supervisor who is not experienced in their specific area of client work.   ☐

REFLECTING ON SUPERVISION

Supervision is only part of the therapist's reflective process. The continual development of the skill of self-monitoring is a competency applicable to both counselling and supervision, potentially utilized prior to, during and after supervision sessions.

Consideration of the outcomes from supervision provides an opportunity to consolidate new thinking before next seeing clients and away from direct supervisory influence. This avoids the pitfall of applying thinking reached in supervision blindly to client work, and allows for the alignment of supervisory outcomes with the counsellor's philosophy.

Supervision sessions do not always have a clear outcome: often the exploration in itself is advantageous (Page & Wosket, 2001). However, a series of sessions without obvious results may be a cause for concern.

The following example highlights how a supervision session can have both benefits and shortcomings.

> Sai had recently returned from a supervision session and was chewing it over. He had taken an organizational dilemma involving a colleague and two clients. The discussion on the organizational problem had left him feeling both satisfied with the decisions that he had come to but also somewhat frustrated. On examination, he realized that little time had been spent on his clients, to the extent that the second had only been briefly aired. He now saw this as a recurring pattern, concerns about his organization getting in the way of his clients. He determined to share this with his supervisor and to agree to manage the time more rigorously.

In the following example, the counsellor Tara becomes aware of underlying doubts after her supervision.

> Whilst thinking about her recent supervision session, Tara noticed that her initial exchange at the beginning, briefly updating on life for the last month, had gone on longer than normal. She questioned if she had been avoiding getting down to the business in hand. She suddenly felt tired and wondered if she hadn't had the energy for the usual hard work in the session. This led her to consider the quality of her current level of engagement with her supervisor and her clients. She decided to make space to relax and unwind.

The following questions are designed to provoke contemplation of both content and process following a supervision session:

■ What was good about the session?
■ Were there any learnings or definable outcomes?
■ How do I feel about the session?
■ Did I cover everything I wanted to?
■ What do I notice about how I was in the session?
■ How was the time split?
■ Do any moments stand out?
■ Am I left with any niggles or concerns?
■ Which of my own or my client needs were met or left unmet?
■ If no response was forthcoming to my questions, how useful was the discussion?

Capturing learning

Supervisees have varied ways of crystallizing and capturing observations from supervision sessions. This in all likelihood will reflect an individual's preferred learning style including:

■ adding comments to client process notes
■ acknowledging supervisory insights, knowing they will be carried forward into practice through increased congruence
■ finding an image to effectively encompass the learning about a client.

Reflecting after a series of sessions

Taking stock of our use of supervision from time to time can be enlightening. It is worth checking progress on previously identified longer-term supervisory or development aims. Most supervisory relationships can be improved with a bit of time and effort if the supervisee resists the temptation to settle for 'good enough'. The following are examples of patterns which, if out of balance, can inhibit making full use of the sessions:

■ reporting back rather than undertaking exploration
■ significant time spent unburdening and offloading
■ spending considerable or no time on organizational issues
■ spending considerable time or none on personal issues
■ frequently presenting many clients
■ generally only presenting one or two clients

- regularly or rarely spending time on broader professional issues
- not addressing specified development aims
- rarely taking observations back to a supervision session.

For Reflection

Consider your last few supervision sessions bearing in mind the points above:

- Are you aware of any habits you have developed in using supervision?
- How are these beneficial?
- How might they have limited your use of supervision?
- What might you like to do differently?

INTERFACE OF SUPERVISION AND CLIENT WORK

We all have our own ways of integrating learning from supervision into our practice, and it is beneficial for each counsellor to be aware of their processes of evaluation and decision-making. Some supervisory insights inform an individual's practice for all their clients; at other times these are specific to a single situation. The discussion about a client in supervision can be stimulating and lead to a sense of resolution. Insights gained can be introduced into client work and tangibly move the process on. It can also be overly tempting to focus on the compelling musings conducted in supervision and lose sight of the actual client, inappropriately imposing supervisory thinking on a client. The dialogue may lead to the drawing of inaccurate conclusions or to dynamics being missed. It is easy to forget that a supervisor does not know the supervisee's client and can draw a false picture of both the client and the counselling relationship.

> Vanessa felt uneasy with the outcome of her supervision session. She had felt stuck with a client, and her supervisor had mentioned a couple of techniques to try. In mulling these over Vanessa felt uncomfortable, unsure that they fitted with her philosophy of practice. Eventually she decided not to adopt them with her client. She was left wondering why she had gone along with her supervisor at the time and had been out of touch with her feelings of discomfort. She questioned if this could be a reflection of dynamics in the client's life which she and her supervisor had been unwittingly picking up on. If this was the case she was determined not to play these out with her client by becoming directive.

As a result of a client being presented in supervision, a counsellor's attitude to and understanding of them may well be altered. Where this has occurred, it is wise to give thought to these shifts in perception in advance of the next counselling session.

> After an apparently fruitful exchange in supervision about one of her clients Carla carried the learning with care into her next client session. She described it as metaphorically having 'a card in her back pocket' that she could draw on if it felt timely. Carla had gained an altered perspective of her client's relationship with her mother. As it turned out the client didn't mention her mother for the next few sessions and Carla felt it would be too leading to introduce the subject. Several sessions later the client talked about her mother and shared with Carla the very insight that Carla was holding. Carla felt a twinge of frustration, a shiver of wonder and a delight that her client had reached this thought, and let go of the 'card'.

How much to tell a client about supervision?

The question of whether and how to share information about supervision with clients touches on the ethics of confidentiality and trustworthiness (BACP, 2010). Counsellors who make no reference to it may regard the contract with the supervisor as sufficient guarantee of confidentiality, removing the requirement for the client to be told. In any case, clients are often presented anonymously or with a pseudonym, making the need for clients to be informed debatable.

It can be useful for a client to know that their therapist has backup in place, indicating a level of professionalism and commitment. Reference to supervision may be in the spirit of transparency or may be an organizational requirement. In general, where it is mentioned, this will be briefly as part of the initial contracting when a practitioner defines the boundaries of confidentiality to a client. Supervision may be described as a place where the supervisee reviews their client work as a mechanism to safeguard both parties and that the client can be assured of the level of anonymity. There is a balance to be struck: providing the client with too much detail may only serve to confuse and raise more worries than it eases. Clients may wonder if their counsellor is competent to work with them if they need supervision or question who is actually responsible for the therapy or feel wary about the level of confidentiality on offer.

MOVING BETWEEN SUPERVISORS

Supervisory relationships are self-evidently finite and will end for a variety of reasons including external factors affecting one party such as:

- moving jobs
- moving geographically
- taking a break from working
- retiring.

On occasions either the counsellor or supervisor decides to terminate the relationship due to some dissatisfaction. This can then raise a dilemma for the supervisee embarking on a new relationship. It can be tempting to be less than completely honest with a potential new supervisor in the early days of developing the relationship. A lack of transparency at this stage may, though, present problems later on.

Supervisory relationships can run their course to the point where a mutual decision to end is reached. For some supervisees this occurs with the passage of time; for others there is a sense of outgrowing the relationship or a desire for a fresh encounter. How long to stay in a supervisory relationship is an individual choice: it is common for supervisory relationships to last longer than 10 years (Henderson, 2009). There are benefits as well as potentially negative consequences to be accounted for in longer-term relationships, as outlined in Table 3.2. It is worthy of note that supervisees are less likely to take responsibility for terminating their supervisory relationship (Lawton, 2000).

Table 3.2 Benefits and negatives of long-term supervisory relationships

Potential benefits of long-term supervisory relationships	Potential negative consequences of long-term supervisory relationships
• Depth of connection • Levels of trust • Ability to be open and transparent • Secure and well-developed working alliance • A safe environment for challenge	• Becomes too cosy and collusive • Lack of challenge • Lack of exposure to different ways of working and thinking • Dull and repetitive

Some counsellors change their supervision arrangements on a regular basis so as to avoid the relationship becoming stale and to ensure fresh prompts to their development (Feltham & Dryden, 1994). A possible danger in this strategy is that these practitioners miss out on the depth of relationship that comes with time. Personal and professional growth may remain relatively superficial compared to the extent of development engendered by a deeper level of connection.

Ending and starting

Changing supervisors involves – by definition – both an ending and a start. How counsellors deal with the normal feelings of loss will depend on individual practitioners' response to attachment, change and ending. Ideally there will be an opportunity to attend to the closing of the relationship, which will be planned and negotiated so individual preferences can be respected. A 'good' ending will ease the transition to a new relationship – which may well be daunting and anxiety provoking in its own right. In the case of an abrupt or unplanned ending, unworked through thoughts and feelings may well be carried forward into the next relationship, exacerbated if the decision to end was not the therapist's.

In the case of a supervisor bringing the relationship to a close through personal circumstances, a counsellor may well struggle to embark on a new relationship. If the relationship had been effective it is hard to adapt and settle for something different. However capable the new supervisor, they may not match up to their predecessor. This can represent a real obstacle in developing a healthy connection. Both parties might be drawn into defensive behaviours, leading to a rupture almost before they have got started.

> Eddy's supervisor had retired. He hadn't settled into his new relationship and felt overly challenged by Freya. He found the courage to face this and Freya was both pleased that Eddy had talked about it and worried that she had left him feeling bruised. Through this dialogue Eddy became aware that he had been 'appearing strong' in supervision, not showing his inner feelings and vulnerabilities which in these early days Freya had failed to detect. Freya was aware that Eddy had idealized his last supervisor and that perhaps she was trying too hard to make an impact. They both acknowledged their part in this shaky start and were pleased to have this honest exchange. Eddy uncovered feelings about the ending of the previous relationship, including anger and resentment, which had influenced his behaviour with Freya.

Changing supervisors brings all the challenges of ending an emotionally involved relationship and starting a new and different one, not better or worse. The transition demands a willingness to embrace the uniqueness of this new situation.

Working with two different supervisors

There are many circumstances in which a therapist will have more than one supervisor to meet their individual needs or those of their clients or organization. A supervisee may need specialist information about working with client issues such as trauma, eating disorders or young people and can discuss with their supervisor where this might be found. Employing organizations or contractual requirements may also mean that supervision provided by those with proven knowledge of specific client or organizational issues is mandatory.

> Sergei's voluntary counselling service asked him to find one such person after they had gained a contract which expanded their client base and resulted in the requirement for a supervisor with experience of working within NHS and NICE guidelines. With the help of his colleagues he was able to identify someone who fitted the bill and was also able to continue with his present supervisor for client work not in the contract.

Such involvement can be rich and rewarding, providing the opportunity for experiencing different styles and exposure to varying specialisms, knowledge and approaches. However, caution may be required. A practitioner is placed, through choice or otherwise, in the position of receiving potentially conflicting input and styles of relating. At best this is illuminating and stimulating and at worst confusing if not debilitating. It requires resilience and an aptitude for adapting to different ways of working. This can be mitigated if a supervisee commences a new relationship with clarity about their expectations and enters into a mutual exploration of how this relationship might work. Thus, a counsellor is positioned to optimize what is on offer in both relationships and to be realistic in monitoring the effect of the new one. Of course, a new relationship may highlight shortcomings with an existing supervisor, representing a different challenge and one which it may require courage to address.

IN SUMMARY

It is far from evident that a counsellor will know from the outset how to optimize her use of supervision. The supervisory relationship itself, no less than interactions in counselling, brings plenty of personal challenges for both parties – as well as myriad opportunities for learning. It is useful to chart the areas where therapy and supervision overlap, and to be able to distinguish the different ways in which personal material is employed. It can be illuminating to develop a range of strategies for preparing and presenting in supervision: sticking with the comfortable familiarity of a set pattern may deny access to valuable insights.

Defining and working with difference in supervision can also extend our awareness: the personal culture of the two parties may seem worlds apart, but diversity can also trigger fresh understandings. Where there are enduring feelings of disempowerment, the counsellor may need to work towards raising these sensitive issues with the supervisor.

The supervision relationship is necessarily finite. Beginnings are critical, but so are endings and the punctuation marks of evaluation and review along the way. All of these stages in the journey deserve our attention since all contribute to the quality of the experience.

Recommended reading

Despenser, S. (2011) 'What is Supervision?' *BACP Information Sheet (S2)* (Lutterworth: BACP).

Henderson, P. (2009) *A Different Wisdom: Reflections on Supervision Practice* (London: Karnac Books Ltd).

Lago, C. (2006) *Race, Culture and Counselling: The On-going Challenge*, 2nd edn (Berkshire: Open University Press).

Chapter 4

Roles and Responsibilities in Supervision

INTRODUCTION

To embark on a supervisory relationship is simultaneously to take on a collection of roles and responsibilities which – in part, at least – find definition in professional codes and in legislation. This chapter identifies these frameworks of responsibility and accountability and points to their application to the counsellor working in a variety of contexts – as well as clarifying those areas where it is primarily the counsellor's personal judgement which will inform the course of action.

OVERVIEW

The type of supervision or counselling being offered, the context in which counselling takes place and the contract agreed upon are all determinants of who is deemed responsible for what in supervision. Inevitably, supervisors vary in their facilitation style, theoretical approach and focus. For some, ensuring that a safe space is provided to 'off-load' and assisting in exploring the impact of practice may be uppermost; for others, safety and monitoring are the primary concerns.

Part of the supervisor's responsibility involves encouraging the supervisee to develop and critically evaluate practice. It is for the latter to respond accordingly, identifying gaps in skills and knowledge and engaging in a way that supports learning and development. The activity aims to provide new perspectives and find ways forward in the therapeutic work, to which the supervisor's sharing of knowledge and experience will contribute.

Table 4.1 provides a general summary of roles and responsibilities in the relationship: it is for the two parties to agree how these apply and can be met in their particular situation.

Table 4.1 Roles and responsibilities in supervision

Supervisor	Supervisee	Shared
• Is responsible towards the supervisee	• Overall responsibility for the client	• Work collaboratively to ensure clients' welfare
• Educates by imparting knowledge and experience	• Committed to reflecting on practice and to deepening understanding and knowledge	• Committed to engaging in the process fully and congruently
• Facilitates the counsellor's process and works to ensure that the counsellor's needs are being met	• Self-evaluates practice, identifies gaps in skills and knowledge and is honest when limits of competency have been reached	• Work collaboratively to create an effective working alliance and a conducive learning environment
• Supports and holds the counsellor by offering a safe space, acceptance, warmth and empathy		• Respect the boundaries of the relationship and the contract
• Evaluates the counsellor's practice	• Listens, asks if unsure and is prepared to consider alternative perspectives	• Adherence to a code of ethics
• Adopts an approach that is appropriate for the counselling/supervision context, the counsellor's developmental and individual needs and the theoretical orientation	• Comes prepared for supervision	• Monitor safe, professional, ethical and legal practice
	• Is aware of context and its impact on practice and the counselling process	• Evaluate the efficacy of the supervisory process and relationship
• Models a way of being in relation to professional and ethical practice	• Is open to challenge and feedback	• Negotiate how best to meet the needs of the counsellor in supervision
• Seeks to minimize any power imbalance in the relationship	• Will inform the supervisor if they are not getting their needs met in supervision	• Awareness of and sensitivity towards issues of difference and developing anti-oppressive practice
• Enables new counsellors to understand what supervision is and how best to utilize it	• Shares knowledge of organizational policies and procedures	

DEVELOPING RESPONSIBILITIES

The needs of supervisees change, probably most markedly during the training period and in the first post-graduation year. They continue to alter as various experiences and learning take place throughout on-going development as too does the ability to take responsibility for the contribution to supervision. As the supervisee's focus shifts from concerns about skills and knowledge towards client and process, she may alternate between a developing sense of confidence and autonomy versus feeling at times out of her depth and being more reliant on the supervisor for direction. With continuing integration of practice and a growing sense of themselves as practitioners, there is opportunity for supervisees to participate more fully in an interactive supervisory relationship with increasing emphasis on discussion, consultation and greater self-monitoring.

The experienced counsellor may at times believe she can manage whatever and whoever comes into the therapy room. Whilst that may generally be the case, the supervisor remains a necessary resource, enabling review and also requiring the counsellor to give account of her perceptions and decisions.

> A counsellor had three adult clients each struggling with living with the consequences of childhood abuse, sexual, physical or emotional. The counsellor realized he was experiencing cumulative effects of the severe emotional distress of his clients and was feeling helpless, de-skilled and depleted. Over a few months, he took space in supervision to talk about his own reactions, was affirmed in his practice, focused on keeping his clients and himself safe, and was also able to find ways of working with each of his clients appropriate to their individual needs.

This supervisee knew he did not need information or advice but a safe space to explore and 'reground' himself. He asked his supervisor to support him through a challenging time in his practice and help him work out priorities for himself and his clients.

As with any model or framework it is tempting to believe that we move smoothly from one developmental stage to the other in an unbroken upward motion. The reality is often different as we humans evolve by experimentation, discovery, practice, consolidation and review. It is possible to be in more than one stage at any one time with different issues and clients. We need to be humble enough to realize the importance of revisiting phases of uncertainty and doubt when meeting new challenges.

ETHICAL AND LEGAL RESPONSIBILITIES

Supervisee and supervisor each have a particular set of responsibilities towards each other, the clients, the profession, the wider public and the employing organization. These may vary depending on the context in which the work is taking place and can be roughly categorized into professional, legal and ethical areas. As already proposed in Chapter 2, it is recommended that the counsellor and supervisor contract the division of responsibilities at the outset.

The term clinical responsibility is often used in medical settings and can be defined as a combination of both legal and ethical duty towards the client. It is a relatively ambiguous term and there is on-going debate about its specific definition as applied to counselling. Its general use in the profession appears to have been dwindling in more recent years, perhaps in part because of the lack of clarity around its precise meaning (King, 2001).

ETHICAL RESPONSIBILITY

This section focuses on describing roles and responsibilities from an ethical stance; a broader discussion on ethics can be found in Chapter 9. As a general rule, the supervisor's ethical responsibility relates *directly* to the supervisee, the supervision process and relationship and *indirectly* to the client, by facilitating the counsellor to take ethical responsibility for their clients through self-monitoring and managing their own practice (Jenkins, 2007). There may be many influencing factors that have a bearing on the degree of ethical responsibility deemed appropriate for the supervisee and supervisor in any given situation.

> Mo is a first year trainee counsellor. His supervisor, trainers and placement organization have put robust monitoring and three-way communication systems in place to ensure that his practice meets ethical standards.
>
> Jan works for an agency that provides in-house supervision. Her supervisor is employed to ensure that all counsellors are working ethically and are adhering to organizational procedures. Their supervision contract states clearly that Jan's supervisor will report any pertinent issues that come up in supervision to senior management.
>
> Patrick is a counsellor in private practice. He regularly takes ethical dilemmas to supervision and these are worked through collaboratively. In the supervision contract it states that in extreme circumstances, his supervisor would report significant concerns about Patrick's practice to his professional association. However, such steps would only be taken after attempts to resolve the issues had been exhausted in supervision and if Patrick still failed to understand the ethical issues and take the action required.

The counsellor has a primary duty to avoid harm to clients, so that evaluating, monitoring and maintaining their own fitness to practise is essential. This involves an acceptance on the counsellor's part that clients may become inadvertently damaged through the delicate nature of the therapeutic relationship. Harm can be viewed on a spectrum, with explicit sexual, financial, physical or emotional exploitation or abuse at one end, and more implicit, subtle and perhaps unconscious behaviours or dynamics that impact negatively on the client at the other. It is important that counsellors understand that being committed to avoiding harm involves exploring any possible explicit or implicit and non-intentional effects on clients, and being open to challenges from the supervisor and to insights and awareness offered.

On the other side of the supervisory dyad, the supervisor takes secondary responsibility for protecting clients from poor practice by creating a space where the counsellor feels able to fully explore their work and by identifying and challenging blind spots in the counsellor's awareness. This process is likely to include monitoring the efficacy of therapy and investigating the dynamics of the therapeutic relationship so as to ensure that clients' best interests are at the heart of the work and that they are fully autonomous in the process.

Jason shared with his supervisor, Louise, that his older, male client keeps calling him by his surname, Mr Shaw.

Jason: I haven't said anything about it because that feels like it might be disregarding his choice… or perhaps not respecting what he feels comfortable with.

Louise: As if you wouldn't be respecting his autonomy somehow?

Jason: Yes, that's it.

Louise: Why do you think he might want to call you Mr Shaw?

Jason: I'm not sure… maybe it's got something to do with his age or his upbringing?

Louise: Perhaps it tells us something about how he sees you and your relationship.

Jason: What… like I'm his superior or in authority somehow. Heck, I never looked at it like that before.

Louise: OK, so let us assume for a moment that this is how he sees you. How does that sit in relation to client autonomy now?

In this example, Louise delivered her ethical responsibility by helping Jason to develop his awareness of how the dynamics between him and his client can affect the ethical status of the relationship. Jason can bring this insight into his work with other clients and be attentive to how such dynamics affect client autonomy and development.

Counsellors have a duty to seek the support of their supervisor, to fully engage in supervision for the benefit of their practice and its development, to be honest if they have reached the limits of their own competency and to take ethical responsibility for their own self-care. (See Chapter 9 for further discussion on working with practitioner self-care in supervision.) If there are any factors present that inhibit the supervisee, it may lead to important information being excluded from the process, resulting in valuable learning and developmental opportunities being missed. The two parties have the task of working together to minimize any negative impact and of ensuring that ethical codes are respected in the supervisory relationship itself.

We have encouraged supervisees, at whatever level of experience they are, to work with their supervisor on any difficulties experienced in supervision. For sure, when there are clear breaches of ethical or professional practice, the supervisee may need to consider taking appropriate action with the supervisor's employer and/or professional association. This could include contacting the ethical helpline or accessing guidance from another senior member of the profession. It is wise to think through possible implications of any step taken which might involve the supervisee in making formal statements regarding dissatisfactions or distress experienced.

LEGAL RESPONSIBILITIES

A number of aspects of UK law are relevant to the context of therapy and supervision. It would be impossible to cover the full gamut of potential legal responsibilities here as the subject is too large for this volume, though Table 4.2 sketches the significance of the most widely applicable legislation. A number of texts which help to demystify these acts of law are recommended for further reading at the end of this chapter.

The supervisor has a legal duty towards their supervisee(s) within the service they offer, whilst the supervisee and their practice organization hold legal accountability for the client. The supervisor would only take action on behalf of the client if the supervisee is unable or unwilling to do so (although this aspect is currently open to debate). Legal and ethical responsibilities are often finely balanced against each other and one of the functions of supervision is to provide an arena for exploring how the two interpenetrate and differentiate. With the exception of mandatory acts of

Table 4.2 Acts of law and their relationship to ethics within supervision

Act of law	Supervision process	Relevant ethical principle(s) for consideration in supervision
Data Protection Act 1998	Safe storage of supervision and therapy session notes and records. Observing confidentiality.	Fidelity Autonomy
Mental Health Act 1983	Working in supervision to establish if a client's mental well-being compromises their own and/or others' safety. Deciding appropriate action to protect client/others.	Fidelity Autonomy Beneficence Non-maleficence Self-care
Children Act 2004	Duty to report cases of on-going abuse of children. Working in supervision to establish whether disclosure is in the client's best interests and to minimize any potential further risk.	Fidelity Non-maleficence Autonomy Beneficence
Terrorism Act 2000	Mandatory requirement to act in order to protect the wider public. Discussion in supervision about how a disclosure should be made.	Self-respect
Drug Trafficking Act 1994	Mandatory requirement to act in order to protect the wider public. Discussion in supervision about how a disclosure should be made.	Self-respect
Equality Act 2010	Taking personal responsibility for equality for all in supervision, therapy and in the workplace.	Justice Beneficence
Consumer Protection Act 1987	Duty of the supervisee in services offered to clients. Duty of the supervisor in services offered to supervisees. Duty of both the supervisor and supervisee towards the profession. Taking responsibility for ensuring good practice and avoiding professional negligence.	Autonomy Beneficence Non-maleficence Justice
Freedom of Information Act 2000	Ensuring accurate information in supervision/ therapy records. Respecting clients' and supervisees' rights to access session notes and records. Legal requests for access to client notes or information about therapy.	Fidelity Autonomy Beneficence Justice

law, consideration of relevant ethical principles is advisable before action is agreed. The following case vignette illustrates a situation in which ethical, legal and organizational requirements are potentially in conflict.

> Dorothy is a counsellor in a secondary school with a 15-year-old female client who lives alone with her father. The client discloses that her Dad has a bad temper and has on occasion pushed or slapped her. The client is worried about what might happen if Dorothy tells someone, but she also wants her father to stop throwing his weight around because it is scaring her. Dorothy is also concerned about the risks in not making a disclosure and that if she does, the client might lose trust, may not return to counselling and be left in a more vulnerable position.

For Reflection

- If you were this client's counsellor, how might you use supervision to find outcomes which honour the client's trust, ensure her safety, and justify any legal or ethical challenge to your decisions?
- Which acts of law, ethical principles, organizational policies and procedures would you need to consider?
- Are there any other sources of help available to you such as a legal or ethics helpline?

Counselling, supervision and legal processes

In situations where the counsellor is the subject of a legal challenge or is facing a difficult legal dilemma, supervision should be able to provide adequate support and a space to explore responses and actions. In the first instance the supervisee needs to know that their supervisor is willing and able to offer them the understanding and support that they need. The supervisor may not have all the answers but by working collaboratively in supervision, the supervisee can be helped to find the best way forward. To facilitate this process, a review of the supervisor's and supervisee's roles and responsibilities might prove to be a useful endeavour to clarify expectations, as would identification of other resources such as legal advice. Some examples of how these kinds of issues might arise include:

- counsellor and/or therapy notes being subpoenaed to court
- preparing reports for the court

- requests from solicitors or the police
- appearing as an expert witness
- counselling witnesses of crime
- mandatory requirements for disclosure
- accusations of unlawful or unethical practice such as discrimination, breaches of confidentiality, or harm to client(s).

Perspectives on legal and ethical responsibility

It is important for counsellors, when faced with a difficult dilemma, to clarify their supervisor's response. In the following example, two supervisors react in quite different ways:

> David's client has begun to work through a disturbed childhood within therapy. Since these experiences were suppressed for many years, the client's issues have started to unravel, leading to an emotionally charged and distressing process. After a few sessions, the client exhibits suicidal ideation and goes on to make several suicide attempts. The client's GP is aware and a referral into Adult Mental Health Services has been made – although it will be at least three months before the client will be seen.
>
> David believes that the client was autonomous in the decision to continue with counselling and that touching such distress is a necessary part of the therapeutic process.

Supervisor 1 became increasingly alarmed by the behaviours being exhibited by this client and suggested that therapy was becoming more harmful than helpful. David felt sure that ending therapy now would be an abandonment of the client at a crucial part of the process. The supervisor disagreed and informed the practice organization who instructed David to terminate therapy immediately. This supervisor focused on client safety and put less emphasis on counsellor competency, the relationship and the contract between David and his client.

Supervisor 2 was concerned about the client's well-being and also about how the work was impacting on David. They worked together to monitor the client's safety and manage the balance between ethical and legal duties of care whilst ensuring that the client was given the opportunity to work through issues fully. Ways to re-contract with the client to address safety concerns and to encourage a level of self-responsibility were discussed. Additional supervision sessions were arranged for a period of time to monitor the situation and support David in this intensive work.

Both supervisors managed anxiety in different ways: one reacting speedily and taking over responsibility for client safety; the other leaving this with David, at the same time as offering him support and challenge throughout.

For Reflection

If you were in David's situation:

- How do you imagine your supervisor would respond?
- Are there any factors relating to your individual or work context that might influence your supervisor's response?
- Does the example of David raise questions for you? If so, is there a need for clarification with your supervisor or your practice organization?

COUNSELLORS IN TRAINING

The supervisory relationship for trainee counsellors can be more complex than most supervisory dyads. Account needs to be taken of the role of the training organization and the placement agency, alongside expectations on the supervisor to assess the trainee counsellor's abilities. Areas of responsibility towards the trainee's clients may not always be clear, although there is some agreement that whilst in training, counsellors alone cannot be held fully accountable. Some training organizations and placement agencies take responsibility for the trainee's work; others consider this accountability to lie with the supervisor. The tripartite agreement (see Chapter 2) is a useful tool for defining responsibilities and channels of communication. It is important that the trainee and the client don't 'fall into the hole between supervisor, training course and placement agency, each believing the other to be clinically responsible' (Izzard, 2001, p. 77). All parties could then be placed in a vulnerable position.

Ideally, there is shared responsibility for the client between all concerned and with open channels of communication. Figure 4.1 illustrates the centrality of the client, who is being actively supported by the various components of the training structure.

The needs of the counsellor in training necessitate the existence of a parallel system. As part of this, the supervisor takes responsibility for holding the boundaries of the supervisory relationship, supporting and encouraging the trainee and sharing knowledge and experience as required (see Figure 4.2).

Figure 4.1 Responsibility for the client in counsellor training

Figure 4.2 Responsibility for the counsellor in training

Supervision functions in trainee supervision

Trainee supervision is characterized by:

- *education* specific to trainees as they meet different clients and client issues
- *evaluation* – as the trainee makes links between how their skills and abilities affect the progress of their clients
- *support* – the trainee being helped to find their way with the challenges of practice
- *monitoring* – encouragement to work within their competences and understand their part in ensuring safe and ethical practice
- (in some cases) *assessment* – requiring sensitivity on the part of the supervisor so that it does not intrude into other functions.

Some trainees in the early stages of their career may find themselves wishing for a didactic teaching style in supervision, though in the longer term this is unlikely to facilitate their development. A collaborative approach from the outset should provide a balance and encourage the development of the 'internal supervisor'.

Learning about supervision

Counselling supervision is a unique, process-centred activity which can seem alien to some trainees. Carroll (2004) is among those who argue that it is the supervisor's responsibility to teach counsellors about what supervision is, how to use it and prepare for it. Other authors (of whom Proctor, 1997) claim that this educative function belongs with the training course. The most effective approach combines both of these, with trainees actively taking responsibility for learning how to engage productively with this process.

THE COUNSELLOR IN PRIVATE PRACTICE

The particularities of private practice mean that certain components of accountability are highlighted. To begin with, the financial arrangement between client and counsellor creates a different dynamic in the therapeutic work, which is also reflected in the supervisory relationship.

Just as supervisors have a responsibility to make sure that they have the necessary skills, experience and training to adopt the role they fulfil, so counsellors need to be adequately equipped to take on the challenge of private practice.

Independent counsellors do not have a responsibility to or protection from an organization or employer. It is important that they and their supervisors ensure their personal, professional liability insurance is sufficient to cover all eventualities. Being in private practice can be isolating and the supervisor may be the only person with whom the counsellor shares their client work. The counsellor may feel the anxiety of an increased sense of responsibility towards their clients – which the supervisor will sometimes parallel towards their supervisee. This freedom from organizational constraints can, by contrast, be experienced in the supervision space as liberating and energizing.

Business and financial matters

If the counsellor is new to private practice, supervision offers an opportunity for helping the supervisee to get to grips with some of the finer detail of running their own business. The supervisor may well set an example in this regard, sharing their own knowledge and experience of the complexities. Certain legal aspects – such as those covered by the Consumer Protection Act 1987 and the Data Protection Act 1998 – have a particular relevance to the private practitioner and can therefore be reference points in supervision.

Being self-employed carries its own unique responsibilities and anxieties – perhaps the most obvious of which is managing the finances of a business and the pressure of making a living. A counsellor (or a supervisor), with the worry that work could dry up at any point, may be tempted to take on more than is appropriate, stretching themselves and their practice to the limit. Supervision needs to monitor this by considering the counsellor's personal and professional context and competence to ensure that they are working within their capacity.

> Trevor had worked hard to develop his private practice over the last two years. However, the demand from clients fluctuated, ranging from his being over-loaded to having no work at all for weeks. He was struggling to cope with the financial instability and so when referrals came his way he felt unable to turn them down. His supervisor was concerned that Trevor was stretching himself too thinly during busy times and that this was affecting the quality of his practice. They explored the conflict of financial pressures against ethical and legal obligations. Trevor agreed to take steps towards improving his own self-care as well as setting up a waiting list system in order to better manage his diary and referrals.

These discussions can also focus on client assessment and decisions about accepting clients. By working collaboratively, reservations that the supervisee may have about certain clients can be aired and resolved. Some counsellors also find it helpful to develop their professional networks so as to consult on specialist issues and research possible referral pathways.

The underlying question 'Is the counselling beneficial?' represents a consistent refrain in supervision and can seem to have a sharper edge when clients are paying directly. Practitioners have a duty to ensure that clients are not being exploited financially and counsellors may feel pressure to produce quick results. Endings may also be a source of concern, since as Wheeler (2001, p. 123) states, '(it) is just as unethical to keep a paying client in therapy when they have ceased to benefit from it as it is bad practice to terminate therapy before a client has worked through an ending process'.

An area which can easily be overlooked is the procedure for dealing with the sudden serious illness (or even death) of the counsellor. In the absence of an agency or manager, arrangements need to be made to inform and support clients. It would not be appropriate, for instance, for a family member with no experience of psychological therapies to take on this role, especially when dealing with their own personal crisis. It may be decided that the supervisor is in the best position to act. In this case procedures need to be agreed and put in place for access to client notes and contact details in the event of an emergency, which may involve liaising with significant others in the counsellor's life.

Working from home

Counsellors working from home need to consider the impact this may have on clients and the therapy (Wheeler, ibid.). Inadvertent boundary transgressions or accidental seepage of personal information into the therapeutic relationship can easily occur. Again, there is sometimes material in these situations which requires discussion. Although some of the following examples could relate to any counselling context, if they happen in the counsellor's home the effect on the counselling process might be quite different.

Consider these examples and their implications when working from home:

- clients arriving early for appointments
- clients bumping into other visitors or family members

- noises being heard coming from the rest of the house
- personal material of the therapist on view, such as photographs or books
- shared personal and business telephone line
- unexpected interruptions, e.g. doorbell, telephone.

Counsellor self-care

Attention to self-care is an ethical responsibility for all counsellors regardless of the setting. However, working alone without the support network of a team can add additional challenges when it comes to the counsellor's monitoring and maintaining her own well-being. In the absence of a manager, making decisions to prioritize personal needs may be difficult and supervision may be an invaluable forum for articulating concerns.

> Teresa's partner has been ill for some time and has recently been diagnosed with cancer. Her partner's prognosis is very good and so Teresa feels able to continue in practice for the time being. However, she may be required to care for her partner at various stages of the treatment programme. Teresa feels torn between her personal and professional obligations. She wants to discuss in supervision how to appropriately manage any potential breaks in her practice.

The supervisor may also feel a degree of responsibility towards their supervisee's well-being, particularly if they have concerns about the counsellor's safety.

> Jordan lived and worked alone. He practised from a room in his house that had been converted into a therapy space. Jordan had been working with a female client for several weeks who had recently asked him about his relationship status, had made some suggestive comments and had begun to attend sessions wearing more revealing clothing. When asked by his supervisor how he felt about this, Jordan said that he felt confident that he could work with the relational dynamics for the benefit of the client's process. Jordan was surprised to hear the supervisor expressing concerns about his safety and the potential for false allegations by this client.

For Reflection

Take some time to consider the responsibilities of being a counsellor in private practice. What might you need from supervision to help you with:

- Developing networks for referral and sources of specialist advice?
- Managing complex decision-making?
- Ensuring ethical practice?
- Taking care of yourself?

THE COUNSELLOR IN THE ORGANIZATION

The setting

Counselling supervision in many organizations, especially in health and social care settings, has historically been seen as managerial. It traditionally includes administrative, educational and supportive functions, all with a clear focus of fitting in with the culture and rules of the organization. The supervisor is seen as accountable for ensuring the practice of the team, 'holding delegated responsibility for allocation of "cases" and resources, appraisal and development of team members and the delivery of a service that meets the organisation's standards' (Valentine, 2004, p. 116).

Working out complexities

Counselling in organizational and agency settings carries the added complexity of corporate or organizational accountability. Counsellors and supervisors may be involved in other activities such as training and mentoring, and facilitating team and organizational meetings. Political directives and financial imperatives can overshadow and affect the whole system. What may appear in other contexts to be purity of focus on the supervisee and client needs may be compromised or less easy to define and contain.

Any organization, most especially those that work with urgencies and emergencies and have suffering humanity at the core of their existence, needs well-defined rules and procedures to cover all eventualities. These may at times hinder the counsellor's freedom of ethical decision-making. Supervisees can find themselves negotiating their way between managerial dictates and their own understanding of professional, ethical and legal accountability.

Difficult choices may have to be made by the supervisee if she is not adequately served by the type and standard of supervision on offer in the organization. The situation may require that she continues to work within a malfunctioning system, even though there are negative effects on clients and herself. The option of leaking sensitive information (so-called 'whistle blowing') has unpredictable outcomes and can be seen as excessive or naïve. Staying within the system and trying to engender changes is a worthy choice, though one which may be too demanding of effort. At such times it is important to consider the option of a move to a practice setting with more certainty of resources and matching standards of supervision.

THE FREELANCE COUNSELLOR CONTRACTED TO EMPLOYEE ASSISTANCE PROGRAMMES (EAPS)

Context

The experience of being a freelance professional can be affected by contracted work with clients referred through an EAP. Balancing the requirements of the EAP with those of the employing organization takes considerable skill. Ensuring that the supervisor understands these different layers of accountability and boundaries is essential in order to meet often conflicting demands.

Contracting for supervision

The contract between client and counsellor and between counsellor and supervisor constitutes another layer in the complex world of personal and organizational accountability. Supervision can be a way of gaining clarity about responsibility for client welfare and safety, to which perspectives of key professionals in the EAP can contribute.

Most counselling requests from EAPs will be with clients for a set number of sessions or even a 'one-off' intervention. The counsellor needs to ensure that appropriate EAP-based support is available and that supervision arrangements are appropriate to the work being undertaken – including access to additional supervision where the work includes crisis and trauma interventions.

Using supervision for EAP work

EAP contracts are likely to present ethical challenges involving competing responsibilities, as the following situations illustrate.

1. The manager of a client contacted the EAP to ask how her employee was utilizing counselling. The EAP then asked the counsellor. Feeling under pressure to respond, the counsellor became less clear about his accountability to the EAP and to the client's organization. He had concerns about keeping his client and himself protected from outside interference. In discussion with his supervisor, he gained clarity about boundaries and ethical considerations. He better understood the implications of shared responsibility and that, with the informed consent of the client (including awareness of any possible consequences), some feedback could be given. He had grasped the nettle of accountability to client and EAP whilst acknowledging the employer's concerns and the possibility of being drawn into client–employer dynamics.

2. A counsellor had grave concerns about her client's fitness to work due to alcohol dependency. He did not appear to have drunk alcohol prior to his sessions but the counsellor was fearful about safety for the client and others. After a supervision session in which she talked through her ethical and legal responsibilities the counsellor was able to discuss her concerns with the client and obtained his consent to talk with the EAP about making a referral to an alcohol recovery programme. The counsellor's conflicting loyalties towards the client, his work colleagues and the general public – alongside fears of the client losing his job – were all real concerns. In supervision, the counsellor was able to work through the actions required whilst keeping faith with the client.

MANAGING COMPLAINTS

Complaints may come through a professional body, employer or contracting agency (EAP) or from a client, client's family or colleagues. The experience of being complained about and of going through a complaints procedure can be harrowing. Traynor (2007, p. 154) suggests that a complaint about a person-centred counsellor is 'likely to challenge their whole way of being' and many counsellors will feel distraught, frightened and inadequate. The complainant or client, counsellor and supervisor can each feel disempowered throughout and following a complaints process, even if the complaint is not upheld after investigation.

First aid

Once the initial shock starts to fade, careful action needs to be taken whilst in this vulnerable place and as the full implications of the complaint begin to dawn. The following pointers to the process are intended to give it some definition:

- A concern about the counsellor's own safety may be paramount, wondering who can be trusted and with what information.
- Approaching professional bodies for advice is a priority. If, however, the complaint comes through them, the person complained about may find it hard to trust that information received is objective.
- The helpline attached to one's indemnity insurance should give legal advice and possibly representation.
- The counsellor needs to know to what extent the supervisor will provide support and help to contain the situation.
- It is important to discover whether additional support and representation can be accessed from a union, from management or the organization.
- Personal therapy may need to be accessed now or later to help work through the effects of the complaint.

On-going process and supervision

It is to be expected that the supervisee will need non-defensive and objective exploration of pertinent issues and constructive assistance at each stage of the complaints procedure. Initially the reactions of the supervisor may be similar to those of the counsellor – feeling shocked and maybe guilty at not being aware of any difficulties between counsellor and client, colleague or practice; fear of contamination by association; and being found wanting as a supervisor. Additional concerns may centre on managing the balance between support and challenge, the personal impact of the complaint, and effects on present and future clients and the supervisory relationship.

The supervisee caught in these situations can use supervision to:

- talk through the experience and gain further understanding of the complainant, the relationship and any pertinent exchanges
- gain as much clarity as possible about what the complaint refers to
- understand the details of the complaints procedure and gather relevant information
- articulate details of how the client work has proceeded and reference this to the theoretical approach.

Taking steps to address what is needed can result in getting a balance and feeling more empowered. Clarity about how to present a response and working out how the supervisor might be able to provide further support, such as assisting in preparing a defence or acting as a reference in any hearing, will all be beneficial.

The aftermath

After the hearing and findings, some learning will hopefully emerge from what is likely to have been a frightening experience – learnings about oneself as a person, a practitioner, and in the supervisory relationship.

Further reflection in supervision will enable working further to develop good practice, including considerations of what might need to change so as to be able to work non-defensively after this experience.

IN SUMMARY

There is a clear division of roles and responsibilities of the parties to supervision, with certain functions shared between supervisors and counsellors. The evolutionary trends in the relationship typically involve a movement towards greater counsellor self-monitoring and increased use of the supervisor as consultant.

The supervisor's ethical responsibility is to facilitate therapist self-understanding and capacity to manage the work: the former therefore carries secondary responsibility for protecting clients against poor practice. A similar model applies in regard to legal duty, with the supervisor holding responsibility for the service provided to the supervisee. It is the counsellor, together with the organization, who holds accountability for the client. Various acts of law can be tracked against the ethical principles, albeit that individual situations may prompt different responses from supervisors.

The web of connections and accountability in training situations, in organizations and in EAP engagements each demands particular definition so that the avenues of communication, roles and responsibilities are properly understood.

The lone worker, meanwhile, faces many of the challenges of legal and ethical responsibility on his or her own, making the supervision relationship key to supporting professional practice.

When things go wrong and the counsellor is the subject of a complaint, the role of the supervisor can be critical in enabling the counsellor to access information, support and perspective.

Recommended reading

BACP (2010) *Ethical Framework for Good Practice in Counselling and Psychotherapy* (Lutterworth: BACP).

Bond, T. (2009) *Standards and Ethics for Counselling in Action* (London: Sage).

Bond, T. & Sandu, A. (2005) *Therapists in Court* (London: Sage).

Gabriel, L. & Casemore, R. (2010) 'Guidance for Ethical Decision Making: A Suggested Model for Practitioners' *BACP Information Sheet (P4)* (Lutterworth: BACP).

Jenkins, P. (2007) *Counselling, Psychotherapy and the Law* (London: Sage).

Mitchell, B. & Bond, T. (2008) *Confidentiality and Record Keeping in Counselling and Psychotherapy* (London: Sage).

Mitchell, B. & Bond, T. (2010) *Essential Law for Counsellors and Psychotherapists* (London: Sage).

Mitchell, B. & Bond, T. (2011) *Legal Issues Across Counselling & Psychotherapy Settings: A Guide for Practice* (London: Sage).

Traynor, W. (2007) 'Supervising a Therapist Through a Complaint' in Tudor, K. & Worrall, M. (eds) *Freedom to Practise Volume II: Developing Person-Centred Approaches to Supervision* (Ross-on-Wye: PCCS Books), pp. 154–168.

Valentine, J. (2004) 'Personal and Organisational Power: Management and Professional Supervision' in Tudor, K. & Worrall, M. (eds) *Freedom to Practise: Person-Centred Approaches to Supervision* (Ross-on-Wye: PCCS Books), pp. 115–131.

Wheeler, S. & King, D. (eds) (2001) *Supervising Counsellors: Issues of Responsibility* (London: Sage).

Chapter 5

Understanding the Relationship: Power and Dynamics

INTRODUCTION

Supervisees' confidence in the strength of the supervisory relationship is critical in facilitating professional growth and developing self-direction. The partnership is affected by the power differential conferred by status as well as by perceived differences and the underlying dynamics always at play. Both parties bring their own personal and professional tendencies to bear on this relationship and it is for both supervisee and supervisor to examine their own part in co-creating a successful and effective alliance. It is as easy for counsellors to abdicate their power as it is for supervisors to wield it unhelpfully. It is also possible for practitioners to attempt to gain power in covert ways and for supervisors to fail to own and utilize their authority effectively.

RELATIONSHIP QUALITY

Equality

The creation of a relationship based on egalitarian principles constitutes a challenge to the supervision dyad, especially in the early days or when there are clearly differing levels of experience. Supervisory responsibility for evaluation or assessment brings another level of complexity. Although tough to achieve, striving for mutuality by both supervisee and supervisor is a healthy endeavour. With this in place there is a much greater likelihood of a counsellor feeling safe enough to be open and honest, allowing for visibility of the supervisee, their client work and therapeutic relationships (including difficult or embarrassing experiences or mistakes). A relationship based on equality provides opportunities for exploration and discussion of a wide range of concerns, enabling supervisee learning and greater levels of self-directed activity. A lack of candour may mean areas of worry and possible blind spots go unattended, with potentially detrimental effects for counsellors and their clients. It is not unusual for supervisees to present selectively and indeed exclude some clients completely for a variety of reasons, including discomfort, lack of trust and respect for their supervisor or fear of the consequences of being honest (Webb, 2000).

> In the early days, Ruth was wary of being open with her supervisor through fear of her competence being judged. This fear subsided over time in the absence of negative judgement from the supervisor and she gradually became more honest. Ultimately she felt safe enough to readily share mistakes, which on exploration led to a great deal of learning from difficult experiences. She needed courage to be less defensive, to manage her fears and to hear supervisory interventions objectively. Without this climate of trust and acceptance, she would have found it hard to discuss many aspects of practice, denying herself the opportunity to raise a range of ethical concerns including client safety.

There is plenty of evidence from supervision research that this kind of supportive, honest and egalitarian relationship leads to clarity, confidence and congruence in client work. On the other hand, a poor relationship leads to a lack of understanding and focus, reduced confidence and less congruence in the counselling setting (Vallance, 2004).

Self-direction, personal responsibility and integrity

If one of the main aspirations of supervision is to facilitate the development of a self-directed and reflective practitioner, then it makes sense that the relationship should encourage counsellors to assume responsibility for their professional and personal development. A relationship where a supervisee is told what to do, rather than working hard to develop their own values, approach and ethics, can be undermining of confidence and personal integrity. In the worst case, supervisees can become inhibited, externally led, rule-following practitioners (Tudor & Worrall, 2004).

Perspectives differ on the place of direction in supervision. Vallance's (2004) study showed that some supervisees welcomed their supervisor's suggestions, finding them useful in opening up new horizons and awareness.

> Bob takes advantage of his supervisor's different style and insights, which allow him to develop a greater range of responses to clients. The effect on client movement is sometimes dramatic. When Bob's perspective and that of his supervisor diverge, supervision still provides him with trust in the process, support and a sounding board.

By contrast, when supervisors' interventions limit exploration or become directive, the responses evoked in supervisees are likely to range between:

- ignoring the guidance offered
- continuing to work with their instincts, sometimes with undermined confidence
- hiding what they have done from their supervisor
- carrying out the supervisor's suggestions or directions, but working outside their values, sometimes feeling anxious and de-skilled
- becoming more directive with their clients.

If a supervisee is able to challenge the supervisor's tendency to direct, then the relationship can be strengthened:

> Helen had the courage to say to her supervisor in a follow-up session 'No. I didn't actually do that because I thought it was barmy (...)'. Her supervisor accepted Helen's opinion and this interaction enhanced their relationship, making it feel more equal. Reflecting on her honesty, Helen reported: 'That's a brilliant way to be with your supervisor' (cited in Vallance, 2004, p. 569).

Appraising the relationship

For Reflection

Relationship thermometer – taking the temperature of your relationship

The aim of this exercise is to help assess the quality of your supervisory ⏵

relationship(s) and identify areas for improvement. Please tick the most appropriate answer to the following statements where:

1 = agree   2 = sometimes   3 = disagree.

Question	1	2	3
1. I feel my supervisor is trustworthy	☐	☐	☐
2. I feel my supervisor is tactful	☐	☐	☐
3. I feel my supervisor is honest	☐	☐	☐
4. I feel my supervisor will not humiliate me	☐	☐	☐
5. I feel able to discuss and review our relationship	☐	☐	☐
6. I feel able to challenge my supervisor	☐	☐	☐
7. We have clarity on and shared expectations of the relationship	☐	☐	☐
8. I can openly disagree with my supervisor	☐	☐	☐
9. I do not shy away from discussing anything in supervision	☐	☐	☐
10. I rarely feel anxious in supervision	☐	☐	☐
11. I feel respected	☐	☐	☐
12. I feel supported	☐	☐	☐
13. I get challenged	☐	☐	☐
14. I feel able to say what I think and feel	☐	☐	☐
15. My supervisor knows if I'm feeling uncomfortable	☐	☐	☐
16. I usually feel better after supervision	☐	☐	☐
17. I usually learn from supervision	☐	☐	☐
18. My clients benefit from my supervision	☐	☐	☐
19. My supervisor joins me in working things out	☐	☐	☐
20. I look forward to supervision	☐	☐	☐
Total	☐	☐	☐

A high number of 1s suggests a productive relationship which regularly contributes to the supervisee's professional development. More 2s in the grid could indicate that there are areas which merit attention. Any aspect scoring a 3 would suggest that the supervisee feels a significant level of dissatisfaction or discomfort either in that specific area or in general. It may well be important to address issues in the relationship to enhance its value.

POWER IN THE SUPERVISORY RELATIONSHIP

Power exists at conscious and unconscious levels in all relationships and can be experienced as a force which encourages and enables or, by contrast, as a vehicle for control and dominance. The balance of power may be influenced by factors such as differences in gender, ethnicity, culture and class; levels of knowledge and experience; internalized or overt sexism, racism and other '-isms'; attitudes to authority; the need for acknowledgement or praise; or anxieties associated with assessment or evaluation.

Inherent inequality

In the supervisory dyad it is most likely to be the counsellor who from time to time shows feelings of uncertainty or inadequacy – specifically in the face of demanding practice situations. This can set up a disparity in power which, if it permeates the supervisory relationship too strongly, needs to be addressed at some stage.

We often start our experience of supervision at an early point in our career when many professional colleagues – especially our therapist, tutors and supervisor – have greater knowledge and experience than ourselves. We may suspect that they also have a magic key to our clients' and our own problems. Hopefully we grow through that stage and develop a more circumspect view. However, it is in this early relationship that we set up expectations and a style of interaction which could ultimately be unhelpful to our clients and ourselves.

An imbalance of power can be experienced as a nagging discomfort without our understanding the dynamics or processes involved. We know that we feel 'wrong-footed' or that something is out of kilter. A more effective power balance provides the ground for feeling understood, gaining new insights and being able to take on the perspectives offered.

Authority versus authoritarianism

The appropriate exercise of supervisor authority can be a significant factor in assisting the counsellor's development and in supporting and safeguarding both supervisees and clients. Supervisor experience and knowledge can often broaden the counsellor's awareness. Very differently, the supervisor with an authoritarian approach will be experienced as 'telling you how to' or 'telling you why you must do this'. The focus can seem to be on criticizing the work of the supervisee, and the supervisor may effectively appear to take over the client by instructing the supervisee how they must operate. Supervisee contributions and experience may well not be acknowledged – all of which can at times leave the counsellor feeling de-skilled or bullied.

> Masie was working with a client for six sessions. By the end of the second session she had a good knowledge of his problems and the way he dealt with issues and relationships. She was unsure how to help him further and said so in supervision. Her supervisor told her to make him set goals and timetables to achieve these. She experienced some discomfort at this advice but acceded to her supervisor's advice and implemented the instructions. The next client session seemed to achieve the aim of goal setting but it felt to Masie that the rapport between her and her client had dissipated and he did not return for his next appointment.

The result in this case was a dissatisfied client and a disempowered counsellor. It is hard to escape the conclusion that even inexperienced practitioners would do well to balance their own best wisdom alongside that of the supervisor.

In the following example, an insightful supervisor notices discomfort in the supervisee and has the sensitivity to raise this:

> *Jane is struggling to manage her counselling caseload in a college counselling service. Her supervisor notices that she is presenting her work differently and with less energy.*
>
> **S**: You seem to be hesitant when you are telling me about your interventions with your client.
>
> **J**: *(tearfully)* I am struggling to concentrate. I've been called into school to see the teachers about my son's truancy. It feels like the last straw, especially coming so soon after my aunt's death. I think I'm finding it hard work with this client who is stuck in her feelings of hopelessness.
>
> **S**: You seem to be holding a lot of distress and anxiety at work and at home.
>
> **J**: It feels better now I've said it.
>
> **S**: What concerns you most right now?
>
> **J**: I know I can manage the situation with school as my partner is coming with me and will be a help. I am not sure how I am working with this client and whether my own grieving is getting in the way. ⮕

> *Further discussion enables Jane to come up with ways of challenging her client's behaviours within their relationship. She also decides to take a few days leave to recover some energy. She arranges a supervision session for her return to work to talk through her level of functioning, especially with this client.*

We do not always notice changes in our own behaviour when we are struggling with other preoccupations. In this instance the supervisor uses her authority appropriately to bring to Jane's attention the difference in her presenting behaviour. The session has an effective outcome, with the supervisee learning more about her own processes and enabled to take responsibility for her choices.

Collaboration and collegiality

Supervisees will often appreciate a more collaborative relationship resourced by their own increased knowledge and confidence. In the following example, the counsellor makes a clear statement about his current needs.

> *Larry is in his first post-graduate year and works in a GP practice with a supportive senior counsellor as mentor. Recently he has been experiencing his supervisor as too directive.*
>
> **S:** When working with an angry client you need to keep yourself safe and tell others in the surgery that you have this person with you.
>
> **L:** I have discussed the safety aspect with my mentor, I need to look at how to work with this client and what interventions I can make to challenge his thinking and behaviours because I've run out of ideas.
>
> **S:** You seem to be annoyed at my concern about your safety.
>
> **L:** No, but it felt as if you were telling me what to do and I felt frustrated at not being heard.
>
> **S:** Some of this could be from your client session and I may have been overprotective of you.
>
> **L:** I want to learn some practical ways of challenging that are supportive.
>
> **S:** So can you tell me what you have you tried so far?

Larry takes the risk of articulating his needs rather than simply accepting what his supervisor had imagined he needed. This interaction moves their process towards a more collaborative way of working together.

As the supervisee develops more confidence in herself and in the supervisory relationship, there is greater scope for self-challenge and an enhanced mindfulness of herself and her interactions. The development of this 'self-supervision' or 'helicopter perspective' contributes to a broader view when working with clients, and to bringing pertinent questions to supervision about dynamics, processes and interventions. This in itself encourages a more collegial way of working in supervision and leads to discovery, interest, new insights and further awareness when with clients and in the supervision process.

RESPECT OR MISUSE OF POWER

Certain dynamics in the supervisory relationship are likely to foster self-reflexive and autonomous practice; others will inhibit it.

Natural insecurities in the supervisee may be increased if the supervisor:

- is over-challenging or over-critical
- overwhelms the supervisee with her knowledge, achievements or connections
- appears to avoid debate
- dominates the agenda.

> Amy noticed that her supervisor occasionally spoke at length about the theory underlying her clients' presenting issues. In one session it used up so much time that her own dilemmas with clients were not addressed. She felt hurt and cheated. When she attempted to raise the issue at her next supervision, she was shocked that her concerns were discounted. The response was defensive and the blame put onto her for being inexperienced and lacking a depth of theoretical background. Amy refused to see this supervisor again. She was left with discomfort about how she had managed the situation.

External signals of respect or of inequality can be seen in how the room is set out. Is the setting relaxed and comfortable or business-like and safe? Are the chairs the same height? Does the lighting obscure the supervisor's face? These and other signs give an awareness of issues of control and provide information about personal and positional power.

The management of time boundaries and the honouring of appointments are important factors indicating mutual respect. Time management within sessions so that issues brought are attended to is a dual responsibility, as is holding confidentiality tightly and not allowing gossip to creep in.

For Reflection

■ To what extent are you aware of the balance of power in your present supervisory relationship?

■ Do you defer to your supervisor, listen respectfully and then ignore advice?

■ Are you the one who decides which offerings from supervision are or are not appropriate when you are next with your client?

■ If you are aware of an imbalance of power, what might you do differently to redress this? (Examples could include devising different approaches to presenting or taking more leadership in how the session is crafted.)

SUPERVISEE ANXIETY

It is not unusual for practitioners to bring a sense of unease to supervision – particularly heightened for trainees or newly qualified therapists. The anxious supervisee may tend to be more sensitive, more likely to interpret the supervisor's interventions as persecutory and less robust in coping with challenge. Anxiety can increase vulnerability to supervisory abuse of power: the supervisee feels in a one-down position up against an experienced and respected supervisor (Kaberry, 2000).

It is useful to be aware of your anxiety levels and proactively take steps to manage the fears and stress sometimes associated with supervision. To what extent is the sense of foreboding self-generated or is it a realistic response to the supervisory experience? The hope would be that the counsellor could share their feelings of being troubled with their supervisor and gain some much needed support. However, if it is the supervisor's behaviours and actions that are causing the discomfort, this might not be possible.

> Habib is just qualified and has recently changed supervisors. He selected Imogen for her experience and impressive array of qualifications. He always feels anxious in the early days of any relationship and is keen to be found acceptable. This is exacerbated by Imogen's personal style. From the outset she spends significant time telling Habib how their relationship will work and is very willing to share experiences and suggest interventions and techniques. Habib tries to conform to Imogen's style of counselling but this does little to build his confidence as he realizes he doesn't understand what he is doing and he feels like her puppet. He becomes ever more anxious, lacking in confidence and he hides a lot of material from the supervision space through fear of Imogen's disapproval.

In this example Habib seems unaware of the impact of his apprehension on his behaviour with Imogen. Had he been more aware he might have taken steps to acknowledge his feelings and discuss with Imogen how to reduce his discomfort and adopt a more productive way of managing it. This would have been more open and diminished the consequent incongruent behaviour. Both parties would also have been better equipped for their future work together.

> Janice enters into supervision with Katrina feeling excited and anxious. Katrina recognizes Janice's anxiety, noticing her abdication of responsibility at the contracting stage, in which she struggles to voice her hopes and expectations. Katrina strives to encourage mutuality in their relationship, consistently communicating her trust in Janice's competence, respecting her thoughts and views and not judging when mistakes and potential blind spots are discussed. This facilitates the growth of a collaborative bond, with Janice feeling only minimal anxiety when introducing difficult experiences and Katrina sharing her knowledge and experience tentatively.

In this case, it seems that it needs Katrina to be aware of Janice's anxiety and take steps to encourage her to enter more fully into the supervisory alliance. It is reasonable to hope that a supervisor, particularly in the early days of a supervisory relationship, will be sensitive to supervisee anxiety. However, it is for the therapist to own anxious feelings and behaviours and to do whatever is necessary to avoid these impacting detrimentally on the relationship.

There are differing views on the extent to which practitioners can expect to use the supervision space to articulate worries which originate in their personal life. A counsellor preoccupied, say, by the threat of a partner's redundancy may be unsure to what extent this belongs in the supervision room. Chapter 3 explores in greater depth questions about the appropriateness of personal disclosure in supervision. If not adequately checked out with the supervisor, uncertainty about what belongs in supervision can cause anxiety in itself.

For Reflection

- What are the different potential stressors and triggers for anxiety which could affect your own use of the supervision space?
- How could you manage these or contribute to dealing with them productively?

TESTING MOMENTS

Raising difficult issues and getting the support you need

It is not easy to find ways of dealing with dissatisfaction or to explain what is not working and what needs to be different. A supervisor may well be conscientious and able and still not meet the needs of the supervisee.

There is value for the supervisee in taking time to identify and clarify the key issues of concern and what changes are sought in the supervisory relationship before addressing it together. In preparation, it is useful to have notes of what you would like to discuss and the questions you wish to raise. The following sentence stems may be a useful prompt:

- I wanted to ask you...
- I felt like I didn't understand your comment about...
- It would be very helpful to have more clarity about...
- I find it difficult in supervision when...
- What is most helpful for me is when...
- It feels as if...
- I would appreciate more/less...

It can take considerable courage to speak to anyone about what is not helpful. Repeating what was heard and checking understanding will assist in defining the issue. Holding the original challenge in a respectful way until it is heard needs a commitment to making change occur. A readiness to disagree and to acknowledge new information or insight can aid progress towards a positive outcome. It may well be that both parties need to assimilate new material in this process. If the supervisor can hear the concerns and respond with understanding and openness, a deeper and more effective relationship can emerge.

> Tony, towards the end of his second year in a counselling post, began to be frustrated that most of his time in supervision was taken up by organizational issues. He had tried to discuss this with the senior counsellor Anne (his supervisor) and felt he had not been heard. He had a great respect for Anne and did not want to hurt her or complain about her practice.
>
> Tony asked for some protected time to discuss the supervision sessions. He had made notes so he would not get diverted from his intentions. He said he understood that the organization was ⫸

undergoing seismic changes which required discussion in the team but he felt that supervision wasn't currently addressing his need to address difficult client issues or his own support.

Anne was shocked and saddened to hear his comments. She was able to admit that she too had been struggling to focus due to work pressures and had unintentionally abdicated her responsibility for Tony's development. As they talked through the situation, they began to discuss together what could be done differently including:

- moving the session to an earlier part of the day so both would be less tired
- starting with an agenda and notes so they would have an agreed content
- taking a couple of minutes to connect with each other at the beginning of each session
- ensuring they both managed the time in the session to enable a brief review at the end.

After what initially felt like a loss of trust and uncertainty around each other's reactions for a few sessions following their discussion, Tony and Anne experienced more openness in their supervisory relationship and enjoyed the challenge and interest the discussion had engendered. The wider issues of organizational responsibility in periods of major change needed to be faced separately with senior management.

Not all challenges are accepted. Coming to agreement about the way forward takes time, understanding and patience. If a first attempt to be heard is not attended to or is rejected, it can be easy to give up the struggle. The consequences of this can mean that the counsellor is less open, less trusting and subsequently more guarded in what and who is presented. In turn this may lead to collusion in accepting inadequate supervision of practice. It can be tempting to take the easy way out and simply opt to end the working relationship, but for many people that isn't a possibility.

In outline, the process for working through disagreements involves:

- talking together about the specifics
- clarifying what each of you is saying
- trying to hear each other
- asking for clarification where appropriate
- coming to some agreement about the way forward – which takes time, understanding and patience.

Alternative sources of support

Sometimes concerns remain unheard, are heard as being unimportant to the work, or else are listened to with respect and yet things still do not change. If counsellors cannot get enough of their professional needs met by the supervisor, input may have to be sought from elsewhere.

Peer or group supervision gives the opportunity to hear other ideas about client issues and ways of working. It can also supply support and affirmation if the counsellor is feeling bruised and shaken. Support and challenge in continuing development activity may be accessed through professional development groups, where again a more balanced and broader experience is available, allowing for learning, debate and enlightenment.

By utilizing a therapist or mentor, specialist advisors such as the BACP helpline and attending workshops relevant to one's particular developmental needs, it can be possible to get a wider perspective on practice and relationship issues.

For the counsellor on a training course the first port of call will be the tutors. They are usually well versed in helping the working through of issues arising between trainee and supervisor. Indeed, this recourse is likely to be written in to the contract between supervisor, course tutors and trainee.

UNDERSTANDING THE SUPERVISEE'S PART IN THE RELATIONSHIP

There is a tendency for supervisees to feel that they have little responsibility for the successful workings of the supervision dyad (London & Chester, 2000). Supervisory relationships are complex, sometimes little understood interactions, with space for a range of dynamics and transferential aspects to appear. Certain supervisee responses can impede the establishment of an effective supervisory relationship if they are not attended to. We all have our idiosyncrasies and habitual tendencies in relationships, which, although natural and maybe out of our awareness, have the potential to muddy the waters and detract from our openness and congruence. Better to consider the responses we bring into the supervisory relationship, and to explore what needs to be addressed to improve the alliance.

The following gives a flavour of elements an individual may bring intentionally or unintentionally to the supervisory enterprise. This is far from a complete inventory, but provides a starting point to help practitioners identify or confirm their own tendencies.

Seeking praise, fearing disapproval or wanting to please

The desire to please and the fear of disapproval can lead to a range of super-visee behaviours including seeking reassurance, being overly self-critical, requesting direct instruction and only discussing successful work. All these behaviours in small measure are natural and appropriate, and a level of affirmation and guidance is a reasonable expectation of supervision. Adopted as a pattern, they can cause a therapist to abdicate their personal and professional responsibility. Too marked a willingness to take on super-visory suggestions can stifle the capacity for self-direction. Perhaps more concerning, these patterns may cause a supervisee to withhold important parts of their practice, potentially neglecting clients' welfare. They also inherently bring the danger of a supervisee being over-sensitive to challenge, resulting in feelings of being criticized or badly treated.

Counsellors vary in their level of comfort when it comes to articulating and exploring their strengths. Nonetheless, it is important to celebrate achievements, since omitting to acknowledge positive aspects – only sharing perceived failures and struggling to discuss success – undermines confidence in the practitioner's abilities as well as in the supervision process.

Being the strong one and having to get it right

For some counsellors, asking for help and discussing difficulties may be a daunting task, requiring courage to gain the supervisory assistance that is on offer. The need to 'get it right' is not uncommon and can lead to super-visees withholding aspects of their practice, or competing with their super-visor's alternative view. Although disagreement is a necessary and healthy part of collaboration when both opinions are considered, this can be com-promised if a therapist is overly reluctant to relinquish their own stand-point.

Acquiescing, rebelling or idealizing

There is unlimited variety to counsellors' perceptions of the supervisory relationship. The supervisor may be viewed as an authority figure, a senior colleague, a rival or an experienced friend. It is sometimes useful for a supervisee to recognize if their supervisor reminds them of somebody else or evokes a familiar feeling. This can be advantageous if the feeling evoked is one of safety and respect: much less so if the feelings are those of fear or foreboding. In the latter case judgements may be perceived as being applied which are not true reflections of the supervisor's view. Reflecting on these echoes from another relationship may illuminate past responses as well as giving some insight into the supervisory alliance.

In situations where a supervisor is seen as predominantly an authority figure, the supervisee may well respond as they have done historically: resisting, defending, submitting or complying. Often responses such as these are derived from a need for self-protection, to gain a measure of control or to deflect attention.

Whilst the respect a supervisee has for a supervisor can positively influence the climate of learning, it can also lead to incongruence and abdication of responsibility, with the counsellor consistently seeking direction from their supervisor. Those practitioners with a tendency to rebel in the face of perceived authority may be tempted to ignore supervisory input. Other behaviours that might alert a supervisee that they are attempting to gain power, erode supervisor authority or deflect and distance their supervisor include:

- hiding behind knowledge and attempting to educate their supervisor
- presenting a long list of work-related concerns
- seeking advice and guidance from a number of other sources
- appearing fragile so as to avoid facing challenges.

Lawton (2000) describes the tendency to idealization, with supervisors being treated as the fount of all knowledge. There is a balance to be struck between respecting a supervisor's different capabilities and achievements, and the supervisee recognizing her own resourcefulness, skills and experience.

The influence of previous supervision

Current supervisory relationships are likely to be affected by previous experience, since practitioners generally develop 'a way to be' with their supervisors. Although this can have felt appropriate at some point in the past, it may also in some ways have been limiting. Supervisors vary in how flexible they are in their view of appropriate topics for discussion and modes of working in supervision. This can range from levels of directiveness to how they view the boundary between therapy and supervision; the use of creativity; and how prescriptive they are about styles of client presentation. There is an opportunity to be seized by counsellors to avoid getting into or staying too long in what could be experienced as 'a supervisory rut' – either within their current relationship or when embarking on a new one.

Perceptions of supervisor competence

Supervisees' perceptions of supervisor competence likewise affect the relationship. If a supervisor is perceived as highly competent this can engender feelings of safety and trust. Alternatively, some practitioners may feel intimidated and too scared to explore some aspects of their work. If a supervisor appears incompetent a counsellor may feel a lack of supervisory robustness and show a reluctance to disclose some of the more challenging aspects of their practice. The supervisor's contribution may no longer be respected, leaving the counsellor unsupported, isolated and burdened by their client work.

For Reflection

- Take time to consider one or more of your own supervisory relationships. List some of the interpersonal tendencies and patterns which you believe you may bring or have brought to these.
- To what extent do you perceive these as having a beneficial impact on the supervision?
- To what extent might they be detrimental?
- Are there steps which you have already tried to take or which you might take to enhance the relationship?

REVIEW SESSIONS

Few question the purpose or usefulness of reviews, yet depending on clarity of purpose, for whose benefit they occur, and what outcomes are required, they can be either a meaningless ritual or a useful and awareness-raising experience.

The thought of entering into a review can be a daunting prospect, however experienced we are. It faces us with all our fears about acceptance, competency, normalcy and the dynamics of the relationship.

Some contracts with organizations require a regular review of work and development goals, whilst others only require action if there are concerns about practice. Students on training courses and their supervisors will adhere to the agreement on reviews in the course contract.

Reviews arranged 'as appropriate' work for some supervisees whilst other practitioners fix an annual review with time protected for this. Time required needs to be agreed and may be within the usual supervisory session. Alternatively, consideration may be given to paid or unpaid extra time within which to conduct the review effectively.

An agreement on reviews – what will be covered, the time involved, preparation required and so on – can be included in the original supervision contract. When a supervisory relationship has been in place for some time or when practitioners are very experienced, the question of when and how to review is more open-ended. The supervisee may also raise the issue of reviews from time to time to help keep them in mind, or indeed may instigate a review if s/he is struggling to find a place or time to raise issues or wanting feedback on progress or development.

The structure of any review can be agreed between supervisee and supervisor. How it is managed and prepared for will vary between individuals and depending on the degree of safety in the relationship.

Box 5.1   Points for consideration in a review session*

- **The context** and any organizational/agency issues.
- **Professional and personal development:** How have you changed since the last review and what are your aims for continuing your development?
- **The supervisory relationship:** To what extent do you feel heard, understood, supported? How do you experience the power balance between you?
- What is helpful or unhelpful in how the sessions are conducted and managed?
- To what extent do you censor yourself prior to supervision about what to bring or not to bring?
- What don't you take to supervision?
- What can you say to your supervisor?
- What do you feel is difficult to say?

These prompts can be worked through separately and brought to the review or the discussion initiated jointly in the supervision session.

*The supervisor may well have a list of items for discussion.

Re-contracting in review enables both parties to continue developing content and process of the sessions and of the relationship. Forward planning could be resourced by considering:

- What would you like to see and experience differently from your supervisor?
- What can you offer to do differently?
- How might you occupy the relationship differently?

Reflections on the effectiveness of reviewing can figure in overall evaluations of the supervision relationship. It is well worth considering what if any control you have regarding the regularity and nature of reviews and whether you would benefit from a different approach to these events.

IN SUMMARY

Research confirms widespread practitioner experience that supportive, honest and egalitarian relationships in supervision foster the growth of awareness, confidence and congruence. The capacity for sound and autonomous decision-making is similarly enhanced. Whilst anxiety is an understandable component of some phases of supervision, anxious feelings may demand active management if they become a consistent feature.

Appropriate use of one's personal authority is a skill to be developed in the supervision space. Learning to harness the supervisor's authority optimally may also take time. When the counsellor needs to challenge aspects of the process, this requires self-awareness, the capacity to listen and to communicate clearly, and patience.

Certain relational traits can, over time, detract from the utility of the supervision relationship, including the desire to please, the tendency to rebel and the need to 'get it right'. A balanced approach to self-monitoring is again a useful strategy in this context. Adopting a proactive stance to reviewing the supervision arrangement can lend perspective, promote innovation and give a renewed sense of ownership of the process.

Recommended reading

Lawton, B. & Feltham, C. (eds) (2000) *Taking Supervision Forward: Enquiries and Trends in Counselling and Psychotherapy* (London: Sage), pp. 25–41.

Tudor, K. & Worrall, M. (eds) (2004) *Freedom to Practise: Person-Centred Approaches to Supervision* (Ross-on-Wye: PCCS Books), pp. 11–30.

Tudor, K. & Worrall, M. (eds) (2007) *Freedom to Practise Volume II: Developing Person-Centred Approaches to Supervision* (Ross-on-Wye: PCCS Books).

Vallance, K. (2004) 'Exploring Counsellor Perceptions of the Impact of Counselling Supervision on Clients' *British Journal of Guidance and Counselling*, 32 (4), 559–574.

Chapter 6

Tensions and Dilemmas

INTRODUCTION

However sound the basis of the relationship, there are factors which potentially inject tensions into the interactions between supervisor and supervisee. The presence of an assessment or monitoring function can place a question mark over the aspiration to achieve a balance of power. A range of challenges can also present themselves from the context in which supervision is offered; others emerge through the conduct of the sessions themselves, extending all the way to the ending of the relationship.

ASSESSMENT AND EVALUATION

The existence of an assessment component in the supervision space can seem, at first glance, to be at odds with the primary purpose of the undertaking. When one person is assessing the other, what has become of equality, confidentiality and trust? Whilst the spirit of critical appraisal does need to be present in supervision, too great a role given to the evaluation of the supervisee can feel intrusive and likely to inhibit what is brought for discussion.

Even if no formal assessment processes are involved, the development of the supervisory alliance can uncover all kinds of characteristics which even the most assiduous initial contracting may not have revealed. The supervisee may feel – contrary to her needs or wishes – that she is too often the object of criticism or rebuke. Alternatively, she can begin to doubt the supervisor's ability to appreciate the subtleties of situations and to arrive at sufficiently rounded judgements. A third possibility is that the counsellor feels inadequately held by a supervisor who simply accepts her version of events, without ever really challenging or introducing other theoretical or ethical reference points.

The important point to consider is how the power associated with assessment is applied. If the supervisor wields power too vigorously, the counsellor may feel over-scrutinized and unsympathetically judged. Conversely, if the relationship is too little marked by critique and challenge, the counsellor may take flight into self-supervision and lose confidence in the activity. Either way, de-motivation can result, with the supervisee bringing few if any genuine issues for discussion.

For Reflection

- How would you like your own supervisor to communicate their assessment of your work?
- Do you feel able to ask for feedback and have confidence that it will be offered sensitively?

Specific contexts

The role of assessment in certain specific contexts is easier to define. The supervisor may be required to write an end-of-year report for a training course or an agency, or to provide a job reference or a summary of competence to support the counsellor's submission for accreditation. It is entirely appropriate for the supervisee to ask to contribute to a dialogue prior to the report being drawn up.

Much more sensitive are those situations where a supervisor is called upon to make a judgement on fitness to practise.

> Mark's tutors were unhappy about his performance on his training course. They perceived him as stand-offish in the group, uncommunicative in tutorials and unco-operative in their attempts to help him address these concerns. They had no first-hand knowledge of his practice, so decided to contact both the placement agency and his course-related supervisor for their views.

Commentators on the supervision process agree that monitoring of fitness to practise is one task which supervisors must reasonably expect to undertake. When this concerns a new recruit to the profession, the supervisor has the responsibility of supporting tutors in their certificating role.

Where the concern is raised by another party, the supervisee can still request the opportunity to make their own contribution to the discussion. In this way, the supervisor has the benefit of the counsellor's own perceptions and experience – which will hopefully inform their ensuing recommendation. It is helpful for the supervisee to find out whether the supervisor will work through with them the consequences of whatever decision is arrived at.

The question of supervisees evaluating supervisors is less often raised, though a training course may request this kind of feedback from trainees. In the case of periodic reviews of the supervision arrangement, there are normally expectations that both parties share perceptions of the work and appraise its value and possible future development.

Even in the most casual of conversations with colleagues, counsellors may find themselves comparing the merits of their supervisors. The reality is that supervisees *will* 'assess' their supervisor and ultimately, if consistently dissatisfied, will make efforts to find someone new.

GATEKEEPING AND THE SUPERVISEE

Supervisees will naturally look to the supervisor for on-going support when it comes to monitoring and ensuring the professional integrity of their practice. The mechanisms by which this occurs may have been outlined at the contracting stage – such as the processes to be followed where the supervisor believes that there are questions about current competence.

The gatekeeping role of the supervisor comes to the fore when:

- supervisees' capacity to practise is currently impaired
- supervisees are working at the edge of or beyond their limits of competence
- activities on the part of supervisees cast doubt on their ability to apply professional codes of practice or the ethical framework.

Experienced counsellors may well seek the aid of a supervisor in helping them to judge whether – say, through illness, impairment, or the waning of powers of older age – they should withdraw temporarily or permanently from practice. Such moments are often difficult, potentially bringing with them complex issues of earning power, status, self-image and life meaning. Judgements can also be clouded by contextual issues: a supervisor who fears that a counsellor's livelihood is at stake may well be loath to state what they know in their heart of hearts to be the unpalatable truth. The proactive supervisee will have begun to think through some of the implications of involving the supervisor before broaching issues such as these.

Life situations can arise at points in a counsellor's career which lead them to question their capacity to offer wholehearted attention to clients at the present time. Events ranging from impending redundancy to divorce to a close bereavement can lead the counsellor to engage the supervisor in a discussion about the impact which these are having on their therapeutic work. The decision may be to continue in practice with a regular review. Sometimes the wisest step is to take a 'sabbatical' period away from client work, with the supervisor acting as the consultant to the practitioner in monitoring recovery from stressful events.

Counsellors feeling outfaced by professional challenges may seek their supervisor's help to evaluate their ability to make an adequate response. Such would be the case where a counsellor is transferred to a different service or client population and feels unprepared for the demands involved. A practitioner experienced in general counselling might feel unable to meet the specific needs, say, of clients who are chronically drug dependent or undergoing palliative care. Discussion in supervision can assist counsellors to weigh up the needs of the situation against their own knowledge, experience and ability to relate successfully with the client group. The key principles involved are the twin prongs of non-maleficence and beneficence: does this counsellor have both the skill to avoid damage and the potential to make a positive contribution?

Reflective practitioners who enjoy a trusting relationship with their supervisor are likely to be prepared to engage in open discussion when they themselves are unsure about aspects of current practice. More difficulties arise where the counsellor is anxious about the supervisor's response: will the supervisor attempt to prevent me from continuing to work in this situation – and where will that leave me? No amount of planning on the part of the supervisee can predict the supervisor's reaction – which could be to place a large question mark over the work under discussion. There are, undeniably, situations in which the supervisor feels profoundly concerned about an aspect of the supervisee's work – and says so. It is important in such circumstances to take due note of the perspective expressed. If, after mature reflection, the counsellor accepts the validity of the supervisor's view, then there may be difficult decisions to be taken.

THE SUPERVISEE IN THE ORGANIZATION

Organizational supervision may be offered in-house or externally, and with supervisors who are fellow employees or independently contracted. The key components of trust, competence and commitment need to be present as in any other context in which sensitive professional issues are being discussed.

Colleagues have to feel safe, and that their interests are not being subordinated to those of the organization.

> Julie was shocked to find her manager waiting for the first group supervision session with the new external supervisor. She had expected only to share the time with her immediate colleagues, and became anxious that she wouldn't be able to disclose openly in the presence of a boss in whom she had little faith. In spite of her nervousness, she had the presence of mind to verbalize her uncertainty about the arrangement. In the event, this was helpful to all her colleagues, including the manager, who took the opportunity to book an individual session with the supervisor.

The example above shows the usefulness of stating one's needs early on, rather than going along with an arrangement which appears to have little chance of success. It is easier to help shape a structure at the outset; harder to do so once a pattern has been established (even if no-one is served well by it).

Supervisors external to the organization have the advantage of distance. They are not on the regular payroll and aren't part of the in-house culture. They may well be able to maintain a level of independence which a home-grown supervisor cannot. They may, however, be less well informed about the minutiae of daily routines and working relationships – and these not infrequently are the basis of tensions and stress. An external supervisor may need more updating and 'filling in' on this kind of detail so as to have a rounded picture of what supervisees are dealing with. Equally, the independently-contracted supervisor is rarely in a position to respond through the organization to situations in which the supervisee is feeling unsafe at work or ethically compromised. There may need to be extended discussion in supervision about strategies for safeguarding clients and the counsellor herself – especially crucial if there are anxieties about a possible allegation of malpractice.

Supervisors internal to the organization have the advantage of insider knowledge, but the disadvantage of being part of the system productive of the difficulties the counsellors themselves experience. This can work to everyone's benefit if there is a feeling of 'all being in the same boat'. If, however, the boat is universally experienced as leaky or rudderless, all of the parties may experience frustration and lack of direction.

Counsellors receiving work-based supervision will need to assure themselves that confidentiality will be maintained. Although some employers demand feedback from the supervisor, this can usually be done without identification of individual staff. In this way, common-to-all and recurrent issues can be named: it is then for the organization to follow these up if it chooses to do so.

The usefulness of organizational supervision can be undermined where practitioners repeatedly use sessions solely to offload complaints, rather than to focus on their interactions with service users. Some amount of plain speaking about the perceived shortcomings of the employer may at times be helpful and cathartic, and in some cases organizational issues can be directly addressed and progressed. For supervisees, the challenge as ever is to bring issues where there is a chance of moving forward – whether in the relationship with the employer and working structures, or gaining new insights and understandings about client work.

Finally, line manager supervision is often not intended for extended reflection. The demands of accountable systems and organizational processes can mean that meetings labelled as supervision can revolve around caseload management and tackling the waiting list – potentially vital issues in themselves, but implying a different style of encounter from the one which brings greater awareness of the deeper workings of the counselling process. The concern is when this is *all* that is on offer.

DUAL SUPERVISORY RELATIONSHIPS

Most counsellors report having experienced supervision from someone that they know in another role or context. This is especially true in a financial climate where agencies are under increasing pressures to cut costs: the provision of in-house supervision may be the more economical approach. Although considered by some as inadvisable, dual supervisory relationships are often unavoidable, for instance where the supervisee's employer stipulates who will supervise their practice or if they live in a rural area where the choice of supervisors is limited. A dual relationship will inevitably add an additional dimension to the supervisory alliance – one which can, either positively or negatively, affect the degree of trust and safety present and therefore the overall effectiveness of supervision (Jesper, 2010).

Familiarity

Supervision has been found to be most effective when there is openness and honesty and a sense of safety and trust (Weaks, 2002; Webb & Wheeler, 1998; Wosket, 1999). The supervisee may feel safer if the supervisor is already known to them, as the familiarity could offer reassurance. However, a relationship that becomes too comfortable can increase the risk of collusion, limiting the supervisee's developmental process (Borders & Brown, 2005; Jesper, 2010). Both parties may become overly protective of one another. If the supervisee feels unable to challenge their supervisor for fear of upsetting them or fracturing the relationship, the quality of supervision will be impaired.

> Hazel chose her supervisor because they were previously colleagues in another setting. As a consequence, Hazel felt she could trust her. Their sessions always began with some checking-in of how the other was and what was going on in the wider context of their personal lives. After some time though, Hazel felt that too much of her supervision time was being taken up with 'chat' and that the process lacked direction and focus. She felt she was merely self-supervising in her sessions and wanted her supervisor to be more proactive and involved. She was concerned that raising her discontent might hurt her supervisor's feelings, especially since she was aware her supervisor was having problems at home. She worried about causing her supervisor further distress, so decided to wait until her supervisor's personal situation had improved. In the meantime, Hazel continued to leave supervision feeling uninspired, without gaining any real insight into her work.

It is important to consider potential pitfalls before choosing to work with a supervisor who is familiar. If boundaries are preserved appropriately and both parties engage in mutually congruent dialogue, the familiarity of a dual relationship can serve to benefit the supervisee. A supervisor who knows a supervisee really well might be more attuned to them and have a better insight into their specific developmental needs. Contracting in such a situation might involve both parties agreeing to monitor the impact of the dual relationship through regular reviews of the process and through a commitment to open dialogue and feedback and to giving and receiving challenge.

Boundaries between relationships

When the boundary between the supervisory and the other relationship becomes blurred, the result can be confusion, intrusion into the supervision space and concerns about confidentiality. The supervisee can feel inhibited, anxious or frustrated that supervision time has been encroached upon. Typically, the conversation in supervision digresses into issues relating to the other relationship or else the supervisor might get confused about what information has been shared where and inadvertently break confidentiality.

Supervisees working in dual supervisory relationships report that the effectiveness of their supervision depends upon the boundaries between the two relationships being monitored and managed appropriately (Jesper, 2010). Although many argue that it is predominately the supervisor's responsibility to ensure that boundaries are maintained, the supervisee has an important part to play in raising the issue with their supervisor if the separation of roles isn't observed.

Concerns about confidentiality are common when supervision is provided in-house. These can be difficult to handle, especially if the supervisor is a manager or occupies a senior role within the same organization. Supervisees may justifiably be worried that challenging their supervisor could lead to negative consequences in the workplace.

Awareness of the dangers and clear contracting at the outset can help reduce the risk of boundaries being crossed or blurred. Who will be responsible for what in the task of monitoring the interface between the work relationship and the supervision space? Where are the limits to confidentiality? How are problems to be resolved? If a schedule of reviews is agreed upon, both supervisee and supervisor have an opportunity to share concerns on a regular basis.

Dual supervisory relationships can be fruitful endeavours, but their success relies heavily on contracting, monitoring of the boundaries, and regular, open reviews of the process (Jesper, 2010; Langs, 1994; Lawton, 2000). In all of these areas, it may be the supervisee who takes the lead if the supervisor does not. If a supervisor is unwilling to recognize the potential difficulties of working in a dual supervisory relationship, then the supervisee may have genuine concerns about whether this is going to be a workable arrangement.

Even when a supervisor and supervisee are not working in a dual relationship, the reality is that paths are likely to cross at some point within the small world of the profession. Contact outside the supervisory relationship often occurs in other professional contexts such as at training events, conferences, subsequent work commitments or due to a shared interest. It is useful to have some discussion around how you both hope to manage this if and when it occurs.

Power in dual supervisory relationships

The issue of power in supervision has been explored in the previous chapter, but it is worth noting here that supervisees are likely to feel inhibited if their supervisor is in a position of authority or holds more status or power. This is especially true of dual supervisory relationships where the supervisor is also a line manager or a senior colleague in the workplace. Many supervisees have reported having concerns about being judged or reprimanded in such arrangements, which then prevented them from being fully open in supervision. Others found that in-house supervision became a 'box-ticking' exercise to satisfy employer requirements, that organizational procedures encroached on their supervision time or that it became insular and lacked objectivity (Copeland, 2005; Jesper, 2010). This is not to discount the positive experiences also reported where the participants were clearly able to manage the challenges of organizational dynamics.

Research suggests that, with the exception of the manager–supervisor dual role, the type of dual relationship is not necessarily the factor which determines whether supervision is successful or not (Copeland, 2005; Jesper, 2010). Although a power imbalance might be more common with in-house supervisory relationships, counsellors have reported evidence of power differentials in other forms of dual relationships, even when they chose their own supervisor. Here again, the success of supervision relies upon both parties having a good awareness of the potential pitfalls, on having a mutually respectful and congruent relationship and by constant monitoring of the boundaries and the effectiveness of the supervision process. A supervisee allocated to an in-house supervisor who is unable to provide the security of a mutually respectful and congruent relationship may wish to consider setting up an alternative, external supervision arrangement to ensure that their needs are met. If funds are limited, then an individual or group peer supervision arrangement may provide a suitable solution (Jacobs, 2007). However, it would be helpful to take concerns back to the supervisor or the organization to work on resolving the issues before making supplementary arrangements for supervision.

Contamination

Information gained by the supervisor or supervisee from another relationship is bound to impact on the relational dynamics in supervision, with positive or negative effects. On the plus side, it may enable both parties to have a more realistic view of the other and strengthen the working alliance. One consequence may be that supervisees see their supervisor as being more human, rather than putting them on a pedestal. On the other hand such information might get in the way. The earlier example of Hazel illustrates the potential for the supervisee to prioritize the supervisor's needs over their own. Likewise, knowledge gained about each other from another past or current relationship can creep into the supervision process, with sometimes unforeseen consequences:

> Tom was Luke's therapist during his counsellor training. A year after his counselling diploma had ended, Luke approached Tom about supervision. They both agreed that sufficient time had elapsed to allow for this transition. Luke later presented a client issue which resembled something he had worked through in his own therapy. Tom suggested that he might find working with this client difficult because of his own past experience. Luke felt hurt by the assumption that he might be unable to separate his own issue from his client's and was angry that the information that Tom was privy to from their earlier relationship had been used to pass judgement about his practice.

It would be impossible to anticipate and pre-empt every possible scenario that might emerge as a result of a dual relationship. However, it is important to have an open mind to what could happen and to be honest when things are not going so well.

For Reflection

If you are regularly working in a dual supervisory relationship:

- What do you see as the contributions and the possible pitfalls of having a connection with your supervisor outside the supervision room?
- Is there anything about the duality that is getting in the way of your supervision process?
- Are there ways in which any unhelpful impact could be reduced?

DRIFTING AND FOCUS

Intellectualization

> **Supervisee:** As you can see, I'm dealing with a real case of existential nausea in this client. It's classic.
>
> **Supervisor:** So you experience him as lost in a generalized Angst.
>
> **Supervisee:** Absolutely. I mean: it's everywhere. Just look in the papers. I'm not surprised it hits me when I'm working with clients.

It is hard to characterize the nature of this interaction from such a small fragment of dialogue, though there are disquieting signs. The two individuals appear comfortable in the relationship – yet the question of collusion may not be far away. The supervisee offers a formulation on the basis of a philosophical construct – and, unfortunately, the supervisor's response doesn't lead to deeper exploration. Instead, the conversation continues on the level of abstraction and generalization. The supervisee may be strengthened in the belief that s/he has understood the client, but may in fact be impeded from doing so by the very nature of what passes between the two of them.

Whilst no universal formula exists for productive dialogue in supervision, it is still useful to apply certain criteria to the interaction:

- Does this sequence support and deepen understanding?
- Is any challenge or forward progress in thinking about the work present?
- Could any future client work be said to be enhanced by this sequence?

There are all sorts of perfectly understandable reasons why parts of the supervision session might not meet these criteria. The counsellor may be stuck in a therapeutic process which shows no sign of moving forward, and supervision may – in imitation of the therapy – become mired and confused.

Anxiety or a difficult power balance can trigger over-intellectualization – sometimes in an attempt to impress or placate the other party. The most intractable examples of these behaviours see supervisee and supervisor playing a game of intellectual one-upmanship, each trying to outbid the other in offering abstractions or quoting references. By contrast and at more productive moments, theory will be employed judiciously to support or to challenge understandings – that is, as an appropriate means to the end of deepening insight.

Over-emphasis on the client's biography

A common feature of less productive dialogue in supervision relates to the challenge of keeping the focus on the counsellor's role and contribution. Whilst it is logical that both parties wish to have an adequate grasp of details of the client's life, too much time spent on an extended narrative may well detract from the essence and utility of supervision. It is usually unproductive to dwell at length on extensive details of the client's life-story

– even though it may have been important for the client to relate these in the therapy hour.

Only over time can the supervisee become familiar with how much biographical information about the client serves the discussion, and how this is best presented. In the following example, the counsellor says enough initially to resource the ensuing discussion without becoming too preoccupied about the fine detail.

Supervisor: You said there were three situations you needed to discuss today. Where would you like to start?

Supervisee: With G, probably. He seems to have been on my mind a lot in between sessions.

Supervisor: OK.

Supervisee: I've had three sessions with him so far. Basically, he was GP referred. In his late 20s. He had a very fragmented childhood. His parents split up when he was four. Then a series of foster homes which didn't seem able to handle him. He ended up in care when he was 10, then was sexually abused by one of the care workers till he got too big and strong and was able to fight him off. I'm finding it very hard to make a relationship with him. He feels very cold, very distant. I don't know where I am with him really.

Supervisor: And you said he came via his GP.

Supervisee: Yes. He's been trying to dry out from years of high alcohol intake. He's been using his GP and the Drug & Alcohol Resource people to help him. They've all been encouraging him to get some counselling to address the underlying issues.

The art of presenting the client and professional issue is one which each supervisee will develop differently, but the fundamental need is to:

- provide a thumbnail sketch of the client with enough contextualizing information to give the supervisor an initial picture of the client and her/his situation
- name the professional issue which is being brought to supervision.

The exploration which then ensues may well draw on further pieces of biographical data, but these can be accessed as and when required (for example, in response to a supervisor's enquiry).

Speculation

A further byway on the road to effective use of supervision lies in the area of speculating about the client or the client's history outside the therapy room. That is, supervisee and supervisor can find themselves trying to 'understand' the client in ways which don't really take account of the role of the counsellor in the person's life in the present. Consider these two extracts, and the different focus which they carry:

---

a)

Supervisee: I find myself thinking about all the gaps in his childhood, and where his parents were all that time. Why weren't they keeping an eye on him? Apparently they were still around even though he wasn't in their care.

Supervisor: So there are all these questions about who did what when.

Supervisee: And what about the other care workers. Why weren't they doing something? That kind of thing can't go on for years without somebody knowing about it.

b)

Supervisee: I find myself thinking about all the gaps in his childhood and what that means for how he is with me now.

Supervisor: Gaps back then and gaps now.

Supervisee: I guess I'm resonating with the distances he got to experience as the norm. I want him to be able to bridge them but he doesn't know how. That's how it feels to me, anyway.

Supervisor: So what does that mean for you now?

Supervisee: It means that I need to stay with him in the way people in the past didn't, till he can feel his way to making some bridges. I can do what I can do, but he needs to trust himself to start building.

Both fragments of dialogue focus on the client, but it is extract b) which truly involves the counsellor and addresses aspects of therapeutic work in the present.

DEALING WITH RUPTURES IN THE SUPERVISORY ALLIANCE

> 'Every cloud has a silver lining'
>
> 'There are no mistakes – only learning opportunities'

How often have we heard these clichés to placate our distress or disappointment when things have not gone well or turned out the way we had hoped? So many times, that perhaps their meaning has become lost. However trite these aphorisms may seem, there is a grain of wisdom worth holding on to for when things go wrong within the supervisory alliance. It would be idealistic to expect the supervisory relationship always to run smoothly – that there will never be a difference of perspective or understanding. Even if this were possible, the conditions for learning and growth might be hampered by such an apparently perfect relationship.

Some potential difficulties in supervision have already been outlined in this chapter such as problems arising from a dual relationship, a transgression of boundaries, a misunderstanding, lack of focus or some hard-to-handle dynamics. Whatever the root cause, when things go wrong, supervisor and supervisee are presented with a developmental opportunity. Being able to work through and resolve a rupture in the relationship could result in a more positive and productive way of working together.

However hurt or anxious a situation has made a person feel, the event presents a challenge to be addressed openly and in the spirit of learning. It is unlikely that holding on to feelings of resentment, frustration or anger in the hope that they will dissipate will be helpful in the long term. Even if the eventual outcome is that the supervisory relationship terminates, there is much to be said for processing the encounter together. This involves reflection, taking responsibility for and ownership of feelings, and agreeing to work through the difficulty in a non-defensive way. This approach is likely to be especially challenging for beginning supervisees, as well as where the supervisee fears creating further conflict or has genuine concerns about possible implications for the future.

Steps and stages for a supervisee attempting to resolve a conflict with the supervisor include:

Box 6.1   Steps and stages of conflict resolution

■ Look back over the interactions with your supervisor. Think about your part in this process: how might you have contributed to the current difficulties in the relationship? Try to separate out what is yours and what belongs to your supervisor.

■ Can you pinpoint the origins of your sense of discomfort?

■ Is there anything familiar to you about this scenario and the emotional response it has prompted? If so, is there any learning you can bring from a past situation into this one?

■ Do you notice any reluctance to working things through with your supervisor? If so, why might his be?

■ What might you gain by making a commitment to resolving this issue – in your personal awareness, and in relation to your counselling practice?

■ Having considered the above:
  – Request some time either at your next session or beforehand to discuss the root of the conflict or breakdown in communication.
  – Remember that your supervisor may have an entirely different take on the matter: be prepared to listen to their perspective without reacting defensively.
  – Have the courage to be honest and open, and honour any learning that might ensue.
  – Decide together how you might move forwards – is there anything that you need from your supervisor or do they need something from you to facilitate moving on?

MANAGING DIFFICULT ENDINGS

The ending of a supervisory relationship may come about for many reasons. Supervision might have become stale, lacking in focus or challenge or perhaps the supervisee has outgrown what is on offer. Maybe there has been a change in circumstances that means it is no longer practical to continue. The decision to terminate a supervisory relationship may not be an easy one to make, especially if the relationship feels strong and well established.

Other factors influencing a decision to change might include a conflict of interests or a breakdown in the alliance leading to irreconcilable differences which may feel trickier to manage. An abrupt ending due to serious illness or, at worst, sudden death of the supervisor would clearly be the most distressing termination of the relationship. Having the opportunity for closure at the end of a supervisory relationship is important, but if this is denied for any reason, it can be hard for the supervisee to come to terms with and to take the necessary steps to find a replacement.

Endings due to conflict

As the last section explores, there can be valuable learnings from working productively through a difficulty in the supervisory alliance. However, if all means of resolving the problem have become exhausted, an ending might be the best option for both parties. It is common for difficult endings to elicit anxiety and discomfort – but a proper ending gives the opportunity to leave the relationship with as much resolution as possible. There is no general rule for how long this process might take – from a single session to a number of meetings.

The points for reflection below are intended as a guide for counsellors approaching such a sensitive process:

- Consider what feelings you experience about endings in general.
- What do you recognize as your usual behavioural patterns at the ending of relationships?
- Do you notice any tendency to avoid endings or conflict?
- How might this relate to how you end with clients?
- What is the value for you in having proper resolution to *this* difficult ending?
- How might you begin to address the ending of this supervision relationship for adequate resolution to be achieved?
- Are there other forms of support available that can help you through this difficult process?
- How do you think you might take this experience and learning into your next supervision relationship and your counselling practice?

When an ending is denied

The ending of any supervisory relationship involves some kind of separation and loss. Even if the relationship has run its natural course, bringing the relationship to a close can be an emotionally charged event. If a supervisor is unwilling to engage in a formal ending or if the cause makes this impossible, this is likely to cause distress for the individual being denied closure. The longer and deeper the supervisory relationship has been, the more difficult it can be to bring it to an end, particularly if this comes without warning.

Supervisee reactions that might be evoked by the sudden ending of a supervisory relationship may be experienced as being akin to those outlined in Kübler-Ross's (1969) grief cycle:

Table 6.1   Phases of grief and possible supervisee reactions

Phase of grief	Possible supervisee response
1. Shock and denial	'It's not a problem. I'll be fine… I don't need them anyway.' 'I can't believe it… It can't be true.'
2. Anger	'It's not fair.' 'How can this be happening?' 'How dare s/he leave me like this?'
3. Bargaining	'It's all my fault… If I work harder then maybe we could work together again.'
4. Depression	'How am I going to manage?' 'I can't cope… what's the point?' 'No other supervisor will be able to give me what I need.'
5. Acceptance	'I need to move on and find another supervisor.'
6. Assimilation	'My new supervisor is not my old one, but they do have much to offer me.' 'What do I need from my new supervisor to help me move forwards?'

Without a formal ending there is a denial of the necessary intimacy and psychological contact for closure to take place. Supervisees may find themselves stuck in phases 1–4, whereby they are unable to accept that the relationship has ended. They may retain feelings of guilt or anger towards their past or even their new supervisor, making it hard to engage in a new supervisory relationship.

In order to move on and into the last two phases, it can be helpful to find a personal way to seek closure. Some suggestions include:

- conducting some form of good-bye 'ceremony'
- writing an un-sent letter to the supervisor detailing all that you wish to say to him/her
- visualizing having an ending conversation: What do you need to say? What might s/he say to you?
- speaking to a trusted colleague or peer who is willing to process it with you.

IS SUPERVISION ALWAYS ENOUGH?

It is important to maintain a sense of realism about what supervision can offer, rather than regarding it as a panacea that will always provide an answer to every difficulty or dilemma. Where supervision is experienced as effective, the supervisee is likely to place a significant degree of reliance on the support and wisdom on offer. It may be argued that there are limits to the degree to which it is beneficial for the counsellor to rely on the supervisor. The aim must be for supervisees to hone their own critical and analytical powers. Too great a reliance could hinder the counsellor's confidence and self-belief, hampering the development of a well-grounded internal supervisor. If expectations run too high, it is more likely that the counsellor will leave supervision feeling disappointed at some stage. Likewise, if there are differences of opinion, if conflict occurs or if a supervisory relationship ends suddenly, then the counsellor may well feel 'at sea' for some time.

Alternative forms of support when supervision fails to meet the needs of the counsellor may need to be researched. However, it is also important for counsellors to recognize their own capacity for resolving difficulties and to develop reflexivity and their own capacity to self-supervise.

For Reflection

An effective method for accessing your internal supervisor is through the development of reflective writing practice (Bolton, 2005; Garbutt, 2009):

1. Think of a difficulty or dilemma in your practice that you have not yet taken to supervision and write a brief summary of the issues concerned.
2. Submerge yourself in your thoughts and feelings about the dilemma and allow these to flow onto the page in a process of free-association writing.
3. By whatever means you can, create some emotional distance between yourself and the problem. As you take a step back, read through your writing as if you are 'another'. What do you notice? Are there any themes emerging? Do any of these thoughts and feelings seem familiar to you?
4. Imagine that your words on the page are those of a colleague. What would you want to say to them about what you have noticed?
5. What do you need to say to your internal self now in order to move forward?

Some ethical dilemmas may require a more practical, problem-solving approach. A useful and effective tool for self-assistance when dealing with ethical decision-making has been developed by Bond (2009) and later adapted by Gabriel & Casemore (2010). These approaches can be integrated into the counsellor's practice to support the development of the internal supervisor.

IN SUMMARY

A number of elements – including assessment, organizational influence and a loss of focus – can unsettle or threaten the health of the supervisory process.

Whether present as a formal or unstated component, evaluation of the supervisee by the supervisor can challenge the power balance in the relationship. Although supervision necessarily occupies an important gatekeeping role, there may be sensitive moments to negotiate when assessment becomes an explicit feature.

For counsellors in organizations, there are pros and cons to having in-house supervision, as there are to accessing an external supervisor: issues of confidentiality, communication and vulnerability are significant. In whatever context supervision is accessed, dual relationships are not uncommon and may present dilemmas when the other connection intrudes.

The supervision relationship is not immune to taking unhelpful by-roads unlikely to lead to greater insight. As a principle, the focus of the supervisory dialogue needs to involve and investigate the therapeutic alliance and its potential to benefit the client.

When things go wrong in the supervisory relationship, a balanced step-by-step approach can lead to resolution of the difficulties. Since planned and negotiated endings won't always be possible, the counsellor can still reflect on appropriate action for the best outcome in the circumstances.

However effective the supervision, it remains the responsibility of the counsellor to develop her 'internal supervisor', so that a measure of reliance on another professional is tempered by confidence in self-monitoring and self-evaluation.

Recommended reading

Bond, T. (2009) *Standards and Ethics for Counselling in Action*, 3rd edn (London: Sage).
Gabriel, L. & Casemore, R. (2010) 'Guidance for Ethical Decision Making: A Suggested Model for Practitioners' *BACP Information Sheet (P4)* (Lutterworth: BACP).

Chapter 7

The Maturing Relationship

INTRODUCTION

> Simon had decided to take his uncertainties about working with Pauline to supervision. He recognized that he had been putting off for some time bringing this client for discussion. For a range of reasons which he only half understood, the counselling with Pauline made him feel exposed and incompetent – vaguely conscious of not doing enough and not knowing enough. His confidence in his supervisor made it a little easier to discuss what he perceived as his shortcomings. As he anticipated, Simon experienced the supervision session as both validating and enlightening. He gained valuable insights into the dynamic at work between him and his client. Instead of experiencing himself as inadequate he felt better resourced to pursue the therapy fruitfully.

The maturing supervision relationship is characterized by features which, if carefully monitored and reviewed, can provide a rich source of inspiration and renewal for the supervisee. The combined creative powers of two professionals who are committed to on-going dialogue and debate can be a significant force for learning and development. At best, counsellors are assisted to truly occupy the therapeutic position which most closely corresponds to their gifts and aspirations. They can declare success, doubt and worry with a sure sense that these will be heard and understood in the context of the broad canvas of their activity.

For these aspects of the relationship to emerge, a number of factors need to be in place. On the purely practical level, those involved need to be able to follow through a commitment to a longer-term professional relationship

– one which will potentially take in life-changing events as well as the usual day-to-day shifts in the fortunes of both parties. On the emotional side, supervisee and supervisor must experience sufficient in the way of liking and respect for each other to sustain this prolonged engagement. Dislike or mistrust or differences in basic values are unlikely to nurture the sort of relational climate which, given the test of time, will turn out productive. Collegiality, appropriate good humour, mutual tolerance, enthusiasm for the task, a preparedness on both sides to develop the self and the relationship – these are more likely ingredients in a mix which endures.

It is impossible in the early days to guarantee that a supervision relationship will last beyond the span of the first contract. For sure, we may strongly suspect after a very few meetings that a combination of shared approach, interests and 'take on the world' suggests a lasting collaboration. Painstaking session-for-session commitment to meaningful dialogue is the only pathway likely to lead from a provisional to an enduring connection. Supervisee and supervisor contribute in equal measure to the mix of goodwill, understanding and energy.

A maturing relationship has, at best, the resources to manage the kinds of testing moments discussed elsewhere in this book. When both parties have the freedom to take the longer view, the pressure to move rapidly through difficult situations or painful processes is removed. An underlying sense of trust and security in supervision provides the bedrock on which therapeutic activity can flourish.

> **Supervisor**: It seems as though we're not going to be able to process this dilemma much further today. How's it leaving you feeling, given that it's a month before we meet again?
>
> **Alex**: Not great, to be honest. I'd been hoping to feel more relieved than I do. But this session has given me some more food for thought. I still don't know whether I've done the right thing by passing on my client's disclosures.
>
> **Supervisor**: No. There are different interpretations of the legal position.
>
> **Alex**: But more than that: have I made things worse for her by telling the school? Did she feel coerced by me into agreeing?
>
> **Supervisor**: And it's hard to live with that uncertainty.
>
> **Alex**: But I know I can always bring it back here, which is what I need if I'm going to be supporting her through whatever comes next.

POWER IN THE MATURE RELATIONSHIP: COMPETITION AND COLLUSION

> Hannah had been seeing Lisa for supervision since the first year of her diploma course. It had seemed like the ideal arrangement. They shared a lot: close in age, similar social situation, overlapping interests. In the early stages, the relationship felt like a well-fitting glove. Hannah felt held and understood. By her fourth year of practice, however, the glove was becoming tighter and constraining. She still appreciated much of what Lisa had to offer and her qualities as a person and a therapist, but as a working relationship it had lost its zest. The unpalatable reality for Hannah was that she needed to make a new supervision relationship – one which would allow her to grow and promote that growth.

Hannah's situation is not unusual. The supervisor who responds to our needs in training may not have the qualities needed for the mature years of practice. Sometimes the level of challenge needs to be higher; sometimes a particular specialism needs to be attended to; sometimes one's own value base has matured and requires a different quality of response.

The danger for Hannah is that she elects, consciously or unconsciously, to conceal her dissatisfactions from herself and her supervisor. Such concealment must, in part, be the handmaiden of collusion, born of the desire to protect Lisa and herself from the presumed difficulties of ending.

The trap of collusion can appear in many other guises. The stresses involved in many a counselling post require the salve of a supportive and caring supervisor. The option of having one's brow mopped at the end of a taxing week of practice may mask the lack of other elements – say, intellectual rigour or growth-enhancing challenge.

Sometimes a long period elapses before it is clear that little that is new or stimulating is likely to emerge from the relationship. Having come to this realization the supervisee may simply continue to 'play the game', knowing that there is precious little to be gained from maintaining the status quo.

The rewards of collusion may, of course, be many. The warmth of acceptance, lack of serious challenge and a cosy familiarity are all accoutrements which may comfortably clothe our daily lives and make us unwilling to change.

The obverse of the coin of collusion bears the unwelcome stamp of competition. For a host of reasons, supervisor and supervisee may experience the need to outbid and out-prove one another – in theoretical knowledge, in connections or experiences, in achievements or qualifications or wisdom. Long-standing supervision relationships can equate closely to those in the family or other intimate settings – hence, to a forum for the workings out of the need to define and identify the self. At the most fundamental level, we need others to assist us (including through resistance and conflict) in these tasks.

A self-aware supervisory pair will acknowledge and work with the will to compete. The use of reflection, shared awareness and appropriate humour can use the emergence of a natural phenomenon and turn it to good effect.

Contrast the following two interactions:

I.

Derek (*supervisee*): Oh, I meant to say: I bumped into Ernesto Spinelli when I was at the Conference. Fascinating what he had to say about a new interpretation of what it means to be an existential counsellor.

Scott: I'm sure I read him on that subject in a journal article last month. [*He roots around on his shelves*]. Must be here somewhere… ah yes. Have a look at this.

Derek: Yeah. I've ordered the book from the shop in the High Street.

Scott: I always find they're slow, so I order online. Better prices as well.

2.

Harry (*supervisee*): I'm still mulling over that conversation I had with the Association Chair at the CPD event in Birmingham.

Stuart: You mentioned it last time. And having a drink with the Deputy. It sounds like it left you with plenty to think about.

Harry: I'm suddenly aware I've been dropping a few names in these sessions recently.

Stuart: I'm also conscious of wanting to wade in with the connections I've been making. Maybe it's worth just taking a few minutes to see what that says about the two of us.

Harry: Yeah. Feels a bit uncomfortable, but I'd like to…

To deny the competitive urge would be to close our eyes to an aspect of many a mature relationship – as well as to a possible source of insight. The supervisee's desire to compete may reflect a strongly felt need to reconfigure the power dynamic, to assert the right to challenge the supervisor, or quite simply to mark a transition in the process of personal and professional development. When the competitive advance is pursued by the supervisor, it may indicate uncertainty about the status of the relationship, about his or her own competence, or about the confidence to retain sufficient power in the relationship. Seen in transferential terms, the competitive urge may reveal a tendency to replay old patterns of avoidance of contact or defensiveness.

It is never easy to acknowledge what many would see as a weakness. Boasting and bravura have seldom gained a favourable press. A willingness to investigate collaboratively a repeated urge to compete – or, at the very least, to work hard in the privacy of one's own reflections to understand it – can contribute to the further strengthening of the bond between supervisor and supervisee.

THE GIFT OF A LONGER-TERM RELATIONSHIP

The orchard gardener has plenty to say about the age at which trees give their best, most reliable and most abundant fruit. Not just, of course, is the lifespan of a tree the significant factor: feeding and maintenance, prevention of threats to its health, timely repair where it's needed – all feature in ensuring that growth is managed and enhanced.

The participants in a longer-term supervision relationship will often, each in their own way, enjoy the harvest which the arrangement brings. For the supervisee, there is the security of being known and accepted. After an extent of time spent with a supervisor, the breadth and depth of knowing and acceptance can be impressive. Sooner or later, what we perceive as our weaknesses or vulnerabilities are likely to be disclosed: my years fighting addiction; your failed marriage; the struggles we both had at earlier times in our counselling career. The willingness to be open, to share the reality of human experience and to use this in the service of the client represents an aspiration to be realized.

Penny (*supervisor*): It feels like this work with your client is touching on some of those really difficult earlier experiences of your own. You've been transparent in the past about what this means for you.

Callum: Often I imagine it won't affect me anymore, but every so often, like now when I'm listening to my client, I just feel that panic coming back.

Penny: Panic that you used to feel and panic that your client feels now.

Callum: But somehow I can feel it and know that I've done the work, done the processing, which she is still in the middle of.

In this sequence, Callum is supported by a supervisor who knows enough of his history to recognize the material which can still, on occasions, feel raw. Penny names the sequence of connections, communicating her understanding, containing a distressing re-emergence of emotion which may well at other times have been debilitating for her supervisee.

Any mature relationship needs to acknowledge the value of ordinariness. Life as we know it consists of uneventful day-to-day working as well as, we hope and need, of the special, the unknown, the challenges and the delights. Expectations have to be realistic: a recognition that today's session is a job worth doing and that both parties will engage with it to the best of their energy and available wisdom at the time. The product in terms of new insights and understandings is forever uncertain in advance. Sometimes supervisor or supervisee may end the session feeling that they have missed the mark. On occasions they will be unable to connect with what they know to be the heart of their best understandings. There will be times when this is brought back to a later meeting, as where a supervisor acknowledges that in the previous supervision he had failed to register significant information brought by the counsellor.

> "Since our last session I've found myself thinking about the client you brought with the issue about his being adopted. At the time, it didn't occur to me that there might be any link with his being passed on to you by another counsellor. I'm now wondering how the themes of rejection and adoption might be playing out between the two of you."

The advantage in such a situation is that either person can return to a previous event or discussion if the need arises. The privileging of consistency, continuity, sustained mutual respect, and commitment to an enduring relationship carry influential messages for the therapy itself. Aspects of the supervision relationship serve as a reminder of what is healing for the client.

TRANSFERENCE, COUNTERTRANSFERENCE AND THE PARALLEL PROCESS

Transference and countertransference

The concept of transference arises from the psychoanalytic arena. It describes a dynamic characterized by the unconscious redirection of feelings from a client onto their therapist. Often these hidden emotions originate from significant early relationships. For example, a client may be reminded, at some level outside their awareness, of their domineering father and act accordingly with their therapist, repeating an old pattern. The response could be subservience or taking a combative stance. It can be illuminating if the behaviour is detected by and worked with in the therapy and usually provides insight into the client's way of being in other relationships.

Countertransference is a dynamic working the other way in the therapeutic dyad. The term is applied to situations where a client provokes an unconscious response in the therapist. Past feelings and behaviours are projected onto the client which may or may not be in response to the client's transference. This can be damaging or obstructive to the therapeutic process, such as when a therapist feels critical or judgemental towards a client without recognizing where these feelings originate. The unpicking of these therapeutic dynamics frequently inputs grist to the supervisory mill.

How does this translate in the supervisory pairing? A supervisee may transfer ways of being from their personal life onto their supervisor and without care a supervisor could be pulled into countertransference, responding unconsciously to this projection.

> Jonathan learnt at an early age to try and please his formidable first teacher doing whatever he said. Unconsciously he perceives his supervisor as an all-knowing educator and looks for direct advice in this relationship too.

A supervisor who identifies this dynamic can choose how to respond, including declining to give guidance and perhaps exploring what is really going on. However, if this dynamic remains out of a supervisor's awareness it is possible that the counsellor's desire for answers could quite simply be met, undermining the latter's confidence. This response also misses the opportunity to raise the supervisee's awareness of a personal tendency and potentially interferes with the supervisory task and process. It is worth underlining that countertransference could originate with a supervisor projecting their own historical material onto their supervisee and not be in any way directly related to the supervisee.

> Emily's supervisee Hollie tended to present in a stilted and extremely detailed manner. Emily found herself on more than one occasion becoming short with her and was confused by this behaviour. Hollie's response to Emily at these times was to feel flustered, making her even less focused in her presentation. In discussion ➡

> with a colleague Emily recognized she was feeling bored with
> Hollie's presentation which led her to be more brusque than she
> liked. She suddenly realized that this was a reflection of how she
> had felt in her relationship with her older sister and that the
> response was entirely misplaced with Hollie.

It is difficult for the supervisee to know how to intervene when the supervisor's response seems unrelated to what, in the real relationship, seems to be happening between them. All the same, the supervisee's commitment to congruence means that it is important to notice situations where s/he feels puzzled by a supervisor's response and, if possible, to bring this up for discussion.

Parallel process

These transferential dynamics in both the counselling and supervisory relationship are further complicated by the existence of the intriguing 'parallel process', first identified by Searles (1955). This is the notion that unconscious dynamics from the counselling relationship are played out in the supervisory dyad. A situation is created in which the supervisory relationship reflects the counselling dynamic and 'the therapist is said to have the experience briefly of being like a client whom she does not actually resemble' (Morrisey & Tribe, 2001, p. 104). A supervisor's countertransference onto their supervisee could be triggered by the client's personal material transmitted through their counsellor (Walker & Jacobs, 2004). If this can be spotted it can be illuminating for both a counsellor and their supervisor in that it brings material from the therapy more directly into the supervisory space. If either party is able to capture awareness of their feelings and altered behaviour, this can promote significant learning.

> Daniel's client is feeling helpless and hopeless about his life, yet in
> the early days of counselling has been unable to express these feel-
> ings. When Daniel is discussing this client his supervisor detects
> that he is being unusually self-doubting. She also finds herself
> searching for answers. She wonders if this is an echo of the client's
> experience and shares this observation with Daniel, which brings
> the client's unexpressed feeling into his awareness. If this hadn't
> been noticed there is a danger that supervision might have got
> into problem-solving on the client's behalf, undermining autonomy
> and the counselling process.

This is only one possible outcome. It may be that Daniel's self-doubt has roots unconnected with his client's material. The challenge of the parallel process is that recognizing its presence depends at least partly on a felt sense, rather than a cognitive certainty.

The parallel process also works in reverse in the situation where supervisory dynamics are reflected in the counselling relationship. In that case, supervisor responses can be mirrored by the counsellor in the client relationship. In the previous example, if a parallel process was occurring and the supervisor unwittingly became directive, it is quite possible that Daniel would then become more leading with his client.

In practice

Whilst it is important to be aware of the existence of transference, countertransference and parallel processes, they need treating with care when creating meanings, as this could lead to misunderstandings being taken back into the client work. It may be helpful to view this type of exploration in supervision as 'playful wonderings' (Page & Wosket, 2001, p. 115).

Supervisor and supervisee experiences in a session can originate from the:

- therapist's response to the client
- client's response to the therapist
- therapist's response to significant others
- client's response to significant others
- therapist's response to the supervisor
- supervisor's response to the therapist
- supervisor's response to significant others
- supervisor's response to the client

(Walker & Jacobs, 2004, p. 48).

Ian (*supervisor*): I wonder if you notice anything about the way you are presenting this client.

Alison: (*takes a few seconds*) Now you say that, I feel like I've been talking a lot and rapidly jabbering on.

Ian: Yeah, that's what I'd noticed and I felt myself becoming a bit distant.

Alison: Actually I can feel a bit out of touch with this client when she talks so much. So this is a parallel? ⫸

> **Ian**: Maybe. What might this tell you about your therapeutic relationship?
>
> **Alison**: I can clearly feel now how my client is trying to keep her distance. This is something I may be able to find a way to address with her...

In this scenario it seems likely that there is a parallel occurring between the therapy space and supervision. In the following example, there is a more immediate explanation for the supervisee's behaviour.

> A supervisor felt herself becoming really confused as Richard talked about his client and wondered if this was in response to the client. When she shared this thought Richard owned his muddled presentation as the result of rushing all day, arriving late and not having had time to prepare.

From another angle, supervisees can confuse feelings about the supervisory dynamic with their client relationships.

> Tanya had felt mildly criticized by her supervisor and in exploring a client shared a thought that the client may have been bruised by one of her interventions. Her supervisor wondered if it was actually the client who felt hurt or whether this emotion was more a reflection of what was going on in their supervisory relationship. When she decided to check this out, it enabled Tanya to get in touch with her feeling of being judged and for this to be attended to between them.

In order for these concepts to be informative it is necessary for both supervisor and therapist to endeavour to find space to maintain awareness of their underlying emotions and to tentatively unpick these without jumping to conclusions.

ATTRACTION AND INTIMACY

Intimacy is a term we more usually associate with our partners, friends and family members, yet the supervisory encounter carries the hallmarks of a close interpersonal relationship. Intimacy is usually a product of successful rapport building that allows the members of the pairing to trust and be open, and entails dialogue, transparency, vulnerability and reciprocity. It is through this very level of contact that a supervisee can connect with all parts of themselves and grow both personally and professionally. It is professional intimacy with time bounded engagements and is to some extent one-sided, in that there is more emphasis on the supervisee being disclosing than the supervisor.

Without a level of attraction it is unlikely that an effective supervisory relationship can develop. We are all drawn to some people more than others, attraction implying that we find a person's qualities pleasing or appealing. The response can be instant or can grow with knowing. It operates at many levels and can be a combination of physical, sexual, cerebral and emotional elements.

A therapist needs to believe that their supervisor can help them, that they can connect and are not poles apart. The pull can be intellectual where qualifications and professional experience bear weight. The appeal could also be more affective. Do I like the look of them, their accent, their way of seeing the world? A shared sense of humour can provide the glue to a successful relationship, as can cognitive alignment (where we sense we are on the same wavelength) or emotional resonance. Common elements of a shared narrative can help people to gel, be it because of life history or work achievements. We can be attracted by difference, particularly through admiration or aspiration. Physical attraction may be a powerful component, but can serve as a distraction from deeper relating, the real person hidden behind a veneer.

> In consulting with her own supervisor, Megan was struck by the consistently immaculate appearance of one of her supervisees. She reminded her of a client suffering from debilitating depression, her appearance camouflaging the reality of distress. Megan was left wondering what her supervisee may be withholding.

Added to the above list of origins of attraction is a sense of 'just clicking', where personalities are compatible. We all vary in how we assess individual personality characteristics and this can be augmented by results from a range of psychometric profiles. These can be one useful way of developing our understanding of ourselves and others and any associated compatibility or tension in working alliances. If one person has a preference for detail and the other for concepts, this can raise a number of issues including a difference in pace and depth of processing. Those who prefer to think before speaking may find it challenging to reflect out loud. Some individuals naturally lean more towards cognition than emotional awareness. Strains can arise if one of the pair prefers plans and organization and the other spontaneity or one prefers safety over risk-taking. Another variant is our preference for relational climates, be they warm or cold (Henderson, 2009). Cooler environments favour the thinking and analytic functions with less attention to the emotional elements, whilst warm atmospheres prize safety, feelings and connection.

There are no wrongs or rights when it comes to relational traits and every pairing brings its benefits and limitations. High levels of similarity usually bring immediate rapport. Differences can give rise to feelings of discomfort and lack of safety. The shadow side of similarity is the spectre of cosiness and collusion. There is much to be gained in working to appreciate disparity with a view to building a more productive association. Perhaps the challenge is to find a supervisor with enough in common and different enough to provide the platform for optimum growth.

In personal relationships intimacy satisfies a human need for meaningful connection with others. This is the boundary supervisory dyads need to tread with care. Underlying personal emotions may need to be recognized and aired on occasion so that they do not detract from the effectiveness of the pairing. The bond fostered by intimacy can facilitate transformative experience and allows for vigorous interaction. On the negative side, it can result in complicity and a deficiency in questioning (Henderson, 2009). Both practitioner and supervisor are faced with managing an alliance which is paradoxically both closed and confidential and needs to be open to scrutiny. This dilemma is best met through mutual mindfulness. Since supervision, like counselling, involves intentional intimacy, the rationale for its place in the relationship needs to be kept in mind.

Touch

The place of touch in the supervisory encounter likewise merits discussion. Humanistic approaches favour openness and authenticity, and at times withholding touch would be incongruent. As we prize contact with internally felt experience it seems inconsistent not, on occasion, to extend its interpersonal equivalent to some form of physical contact. This does not mean that the use of touch is ever treated lightly, since mutual respect and appreciation of difference is also a common denominator. There are many benefits to using touch, which embodies genuine person-to-person bonding, encourages intimacy and can provide physical containment, tangible grounding and felt support.

> On seeing his supervisor, Sian, for the first time since he received the positive news that his accreditation application had been successful, Andrew found himself enveloped in an enormous hug from her and with enthusiastic words of congratulation ringing in his ears. Although taken aback at first he found himself hugging back, and a warm feeling of pleasure and pride rose up in him. Later in the session Sian checked how it had been for this level of physical contact to take place. Andrew was able to share that genuinely feeling Sian's delight for him had helped him to connect with his own feelings of achievement.

It is not unusual in close professional relationships for touch to figure naturally, be it a handshake, a hand to the shoulder, or hugging on meeting or leaving. It becomes harmful when associated with sexuality or when the meaning behind it is unclear to one or both parties. Some of us are more 'touchy feely' than others, offering and seeking reassurance through touch. There are those who find physical contact uncomfortable and intrusive. When touch is misunderstood and non-reciprocal this can create distance and disparity in power or else indicate the start of a slip from a professional to a more personal association.

Interpretation of touch is influenced by a myriad of factors including culture, gender, age, personal preference and history. Any downside to its use can only be explored through open dialogue when touch is on offer or has occurred (Tune, 2005). Supervisory pairs need to be robust enough to handle a difference in preference without either person feeling let down or going along with an activity grudgingly. Spontaneous touch or a fleeting urge to make contact could, of course, be rooted in the therapeutic enterprise: examining its use in supervision can make a positive contribution to proficient practice.

Sexual attraction

Sexual attraction is potentially present in all relationships including therapy and supervision and needs to be recognized so that it can be appropriately managed. Through exploration much information and learning can be gleaned. Sexual attraction between a supervisee and supervisor can derive from a variety of sources, including responses to client work and to personal life situations. It may constitute a strategy to avoid uncomfortable feelings such as anxiety or to maintain a distance. It is the responsibility of both parties to look out for and attend to any such experiences. Martin et al. (2011) propose the following steps:

1. Noticing any sexual feelings or longings both in the session and outwith.
2. Facing up to these experiences – which can be difficult as they often evoke embarrassment.
3. Reflecting on the origins of these feelings (current or past relationships).
4. Processing to better understand any consequences.
5. Formulating how to use this experience for the best professional benefit.

For Reflection

- What do you like and find attractive about your supervisor?
- Are you aware of any behaviours you adopt to be more likeable or attractive in supervision?
- How might your answers impact on your relationship both positively and detrimentally?

THE TRANSPERSONAL IN SUPERVISION

The previous section cites elements of the relationship – including physical attractiveness and the use of touch – which, with a good measure of self-awareness, can be named and brought more fully into consciousness. Other components may escape our attention for longer.

Authors on the unconscious elements in supervision are sometimes (as with Gilbert & Evans, 2000) prepared to extend their perspective to what are variously termed transpersonal, intuitive or spiritual aspects. Seen through these lenses, the supervision relationship operates just as powerfully out of as within the awareness of the participants.

At the basic level of perception and mutual understanding, any longer-term relationship quite simply provides more data. Fellow travellers learn over time about each other's favoured responses, values and preferences, which do not have to be overtly shared to become familiar. Since familiarity – so runs the adage – also breeds contempt, the responsibility of supervisor and supervisee is to monitor how these inform the alliance, enhancing or restricting its power.

Laura had found it difficult to define what no longer worked for her with a supervisor well known in the profession for his skill and experience. A hiatus in the supervisor's availability put her in touch ➡

> with a new supervisor, with whom she felt differently. Difficult though it was to define, the new relationship corresponded much more closely to her sense of herself as a person: spontaneous, creative, willing to take appropriate risks. She grew the wings she needed to fly, deftly supported by a supervisor who seemed, early on, to sense her need to be given the space to experiment, to find her own way of being and doing in the therapeutic space.

The mature relationship in supervision has the potential to provide access to elements of the transpersonal in a way which shorter-term engagements are unlikely to do. Predictably, any attempt to describe what is meant by this component risks foundering on the twin rocks of incomprehension and scepticism. Those aspects of human experience which Jung sought to capture – and which terms such as transcendent, spiritual or 'the soul' try, however inadequately, to define – run uncomfortably counter to much that our culture is about (Rowan, 1993). It is not so exotic, though, to discuss concepts of relational depth, or of client–counsellor fit, or of the search for meaning in psychotherapeutic work.

The patient construction of a relationship with a supervisor over months or years can bring a closeness and a set of mutual understandings which allows communication on the level implied by these terms. If as therapists we hold to the hope of a deeper, more meaningful contact with at least some of our clients, why should we not expect supervision to be a forum in which this is also experienced?

The sea of connections between two professionals is composed of a swim of attitudes, emotions, images, wonderings, spaces between the words. The environment may come to feel hospitable or hostile, welcoming of rumination on practice, or critical and limiting. Where the practitioner's sense of the human endeavour takes in the transpersonal, supervision too will need to offer an openness to this element, to felt understandings, an assumption of not knowing, an awareness of the numinous.

Intuition

The concept of intuitive knowing may be easier for many people to accept than notions of the spiritual. Most will acknowledge the existence of understandings or awareness that we cannot rationally justify – those which go beyond obvious comprehension and the limitations of cognitive thinking. Intuitive processes can be productive of creativity and innovation, generating perceptive and frequently accurate insights. They are prized in humanistic-integrative supervision along with the willingness to work with not knowing and uncertainty. Illumination and learning can be achieved in supervision which allows for mutual exploration of feelings, metaphors and hunches, setting aside the impulse to reach fixed outcomes and appraising all possibilities tentatively.

> **Steve:** As I sit here now talking about this client I feel really sad, lost and kind of isolated.
>
> **Wendy:** A sense of being on your own.
>
> **Steve:** Yeah, and I guess some of this is how my client feels although she hasn't actually said that.
>
> **Wendy:** So some of the sadness and isolation might be your client's.
>
> **Steve:** And some of it is mine. I've only just realized what part of the bond might be about.

Both supervisor and supervisee allow themselves to experience and articulate feelings which cast light on one of the strands of the therapeutic alliance. Openly sharing impressions, thoughts and feelings can lead to possibilities of understanding which cognitive analysis alone may be insufficiently resourced to achieve.

> **Bella:** I feel I'm missing something with this client.
>
> **Keith:** Something missing. Can you say any more?
>
> **Bella:** Something I'm not seeing or that the client is hiding.
>
> **Keith:** I notice you've put your hand to your chest.
>
> **Bella:** I feel sort of empty, like I've lost something.
>
> **Keith:** Something missing and something lost.
>
> **Bella:** My hunch is my client is avoiding talking about some significant loss.

At this point, Bella's hunch is no more than a hypothesis. Intriguingly, though, her client broaches the subject of her still-born baby in the next session.

These kinds of occurrence remind us that we are asking of our supervisor no more than we ask of ourselves as therapists: to be accessible to the range of sensory and imaginal experiences – to note and be prepared to work with what lies at the margins of awareness.

PREPARING FOR ACCREDITATION

The final section of this chapter discusses what might seem to be a purely practical milestone. Yet embedded in this event, if it is to be meaningful, are discussions in supervision about the characteristics which make the counsellor's work most effective and personally valid. Accredited membership of a professional body has developed to become an integral part of the drive towards further professionalism of the therapy field. Practitioners aspire to accredited status for a number of reasons, including its confirming their maturity as professionals and enhancing career options.

Most procedures leading to accreditation involve the practitioner in preparing an extensive application (sometimes phased) and, with selected bodies, attending for interview. An impressive collection of documentary evidence is normally required, including a supervisor's report. Where guidance on the process is available, as with BACP, the accrediting body suggests collaborative supervisory involvement, including discussions on readiness, review of practice, and reflections on philosophy and ethics (BACP, 2012b).

Frequently the preparation period involves activity spanning many months. The supervisee will need to decide how much time in supervision to spend in accreditation-related discussions, whilst not losing sight of current clients. It can be an emotional road on which counsellors can feel exposed and anxious as they strive to articulate their practice and receive their supervisor's feedback both verbally and in a written report. Whilst we know there is always more to learn, it can still be daunting to hear about areas for development. All of this is prior to sending off the completed submission for assessment, waiting for the response and, in the worst case, needing to resubmit.

For some supervisory dyads it may be years since any type of formal assessment has entered the supervisory space, making for unsettling feelings in an established collegial pairing. Inevitably power dynamics will raise their head and will need attention. There is also the responsibility to avoid collusion through laziness or mutual appreciation.

Generally, it is advisable and beneficial to share drafts and receive supervisory feedback at an early stage. Supervisees usually find this delivers the most learning and improves the quality of the application. Most therapists find the process ultimately rewarding: that it enhances their competence and confidence, and conveys a sense of 'I really know what I'm doing'. They enjoy the affirmation afforded them by gaining the approval of their professional body.

There are, though, potential pitfalls to be negotiated. What if a supervisor has doubts about their supervisee's readiness? By committing to write a report they are implicitly endorsing the application. What if a supervisee is disappointed with their supervisor's report or feedback on their application? These and similar situations require careful handling to reach an accord on developmental gaps and appropriate timescales. The quality and safety of the supervisory relationship clearly makes a difference to how supported a supervisee might feel.

> **Bipin:** Thank you for your supervisor's report. It reads well and I'm happy with it all except one bit. You write that I am becoming conversant with the ethical framework and that feels a bit unfair. I do know it and use it regularly.
>
> **Debbie:** Can we just check our understanding here. It may be we have different views on this or I may have worded that sentence clumsily.
>
> **Bipin:** That would be good. What did you mean?
>
> **Debbie:** I was trying to accurately reflect your familiarity and use of the framework. We have worked with it a few times in here. However, sometimes I find myself prompting you to consider it in some of your client work.
>
> **Bipin:** OK. So what you are saying is I do know it and use it and could access it even more. When I read your report I thought you meant I rarely referred to it.
>
> **Debbie:** That's not what I intended. It sounds like we have a better understanding. Could it be worded better?
>
> **Bipin:** Um, maybe 'increasingly conversant' would feel more accurate…

Some supervisees lacking insight into their areas for development may find feedback of this kind difficult to take on board, exacerbated if it has not been raised before by the supervisor (Henderson, 2009). It is worth remembering that supervisors vary in their ability to provide feedback and in their way of giving it. Supervisees may benefit from focusing on what is said for what they can learn rather than hearing it as criticism.

Another possible area of contention arises when there is a difference of opinion on the counsellor's practice, which can be for a range of reasons:

■ The supervisor does not have an accurate view of their supervisee's way of working.

■ The supervisee has failed to clearly communicate their practice.

■ The supervisee has not been fully authentic in describing their practice in their application.

On occasions divergence of views could be more deep seated. This can arise where there are conflicting beliefs and the supervisor feels unable to support part of their supervisee's practice.

> **Rosie**: Reading your case study I was surprised to find that some of your counselling sessions took place in the client's home and not at the counselling service. I supervised this work and this is the first I knew of this.
>
> **Catherine**: I never felt the need to discuss it. My client requests me to see her at home from time to time and so I do. One of my colleagues does it regularly.
>
> **Rosie**: You haven't felt the need to weigh up any consequences on the therapeutic work?
>
> **Catherine**: As you know I work in a person-centred way and I was taking my client's lead. What do you mean by consequences?
>
> **Rosie**: I guess I mean changes to boundaries, contracting, maybe insurance even.
>
> **Catherine**: So you're saying I should never act spontaneously.

The apparent disparity of values evidenced in this snippet of dialogue represents a challenge to be worked with. With goodwill on both sides, situations like this can be resolved. The aim is to avoid an erosion of trust in the relationship from which, in rare circumstances, the supervisory dyad cannot recover. Chapter 5 deals in some detail with handling such difficult times.

On a brighter note, the rewards from successfully navigating this complex process should leave the practitioner feeling refreshed and enjoying the affirmation received from the written supervisor's report, a precious validation in such an isolated profession. Overall, the whole enterprise can be eased if a counsellor adopts an attitude of self-acceptance, tolerance and patience. The challenges it presents can be both stimulating and perplexing, and it is worth considering seeking other forms of support beyond the contribution of your supervisor. Discussion with colleagues who are preparing or have completed their own submission can be fruitful. Professional bodies often offer workshops and helplines to augment their written guidelines.

As significant as the moment of accreditation is for any practitioner, it is worth remembering that it represents a stage of professional development and not an end point. The journey of supervision continues, and should be enhanced and enriched by mutual engagement in this process.

IN SUMMARY

It is impossible to predict whether a supervisory pairing will develop productively in the longer term, though the counsellor's input of tolerance and commitment will contribute to its quality and longevity. If appropriately harnessed, the long-term relationship can offer depth of understanding and the fruits of shared experience.

The identification of transference reactions provides a resource to extend the practitioner's awareness of the dynamics in the therapy and in the supervisory dyad. Noting the existence of 'parallel process' can likewise shed light on puzzling interactions – and prevent a repetition with clients of unhelpful patterns of response.

The intimacy of a long-term professional relationship can provide great benefits where it operates in an atmosphere of security, trust and non-defensiveness. Transpersonal elements may be both valuable and influential. The capacity to work at the margins of awareness (for example with hunches, intuition and a 'felt sense') is an important feature.

A number of elements come together in the run-up to accreditation, with the counsellor needing good quality feedback from a supervisor informed about the detail of her practice and who can effectively support and critique the application.

Recommended reading

Henderson, P. (2009) *A Different Wisdom: Reflections on Supervision Practice* (London: Karnac Books Ltd).

Mearns, D. & Cooper, M. (2005) *Working at Relational Depth* (London: Sage).

Shohet, R. (ed.) (2008) *Passionate Supervision* (London: Jessica Kingsley Publishers).

Shohet, R. (ed.) (2011) *Supervision as Transformation: A Passion for Learning* (London: Jessica Kingsley Publishers).

Chapter 8

Extending the Scope of Supervision

INTRODUCTION

This chapter extends the scope of possibilities by reviewing group, peer and creative methods of using supervision and considers the benefits and challenges of the use of alternative channels such as telephone, skype and the internet, dealing throughout with ethical considerations in a world of constantly changing media.

GROUP SUPERVISION

Group supervision can be a remarkable forum for hearing diverse perspectives and experiencing different approaches. The opportunities for exchange of ideas and experiences are unbounded. Balanced against these advantages, the complexity of material that enters and occurs in the group's world and the management of interactions between members can affect individuals and the group in unhelpful ways. Table 8.1, drawing on Carroll (2004), defines some of the benefits and limitations of supervision in a group setting.

The four main types of supervision group can be summarized as:

- **authoritative:** where a facilitator manages the group and supervises individuals with other group members as audience
- **participative:** where the facilitator supervises and encourages participation from other members
- **co-operative:** in which the supervisor facilitates learning and helps members to take a part in the responsibilities involved in supervising each other

■ **peer:** where each person shares responsibility for supervising, structuring time, monitoring practice and developing the success or otherwise of the group (Proctor, 2008).

Any of the above can develop from one type of group to another or combine two styles as members gain experience in supervision, knowledge and skills. Where this occurs, acknowledgement of the changes and revisiting of roles and responsibilities is essential.

Table 8.1   Group setting strengths and limitations

Strengths	Limitations
• Working with colleagues with different counselling theories and experiences	• Difficulties balancing group and individual needs: group needs may dominate
• Hearing how others (not only the supervisor) work with therapeutic problems	• Effects of having group members at different developmental stages. Those with less experience may feel intimidated and those with more may put their needs last
• Mutual support and encouragement	• Group dynamics can affect the learning climate. Competition, scapegoating or rivalry can be present
• The opportunity for feedback from a number of people, so gaining a more rounded understanding of self	• There might be less time for exploration, experimentation and discovery
• Contact with issues that affect others in the workplace or service	• Possible danger of overload due to amount of work brought by members
• A wider referral network than in one-to-one supervision	• Organizational aspects may impinge on supervision time
• Cost-effective in time and finance	• Reluctance to challenge or face unhelpful behaviours by leaving that responsibility to the supervisor/facilitator

Group tasks and practicalities

Throughout the life of a group the tasks of supervision can be identified as:

■ managing supervision of client work
■ building, maintaining and repairing a working group alliance
■ supporting and challenging individuals to develop and take responsibility for their on-going work management and professional development.

The accountability for these tasks and for group cohesion belongs to each individual even if a facilitator provides the overall framework. It is an obligation on each person to be aware of how their input and way of being in the sessions affect the group's activity and dynamics. Encouraging and challenging other members and accepting challenge from them will go a long way towards ensuring development in oneself and others.

Finding the group to suit you

Even with an agreed group contract, planning for how it will work in practice is not straightforward. Forging working alliances takes time and commitment to the activity and the group. If a choice of groups is available, the list in Box 8.1 could inform a decision to join or not. If no such choice exists, the points identified still need to be addressed at the contracting stage.

Box 8.1   Aspects to consider before joining a group

- Size of group and ensuring sufficient time is available for each member
- Is the group open or closed, fixed term or on-going? How does it manage beginnings and endings?
- The level of experience of participants and the possible effects of a mix
- Frequency and duration of meetings and attendance requirements
- Which theoretical approach, models and frameworks will be used?
- Responsibilities of members and facilitator
- How is confidentiality agreed and held within the group?
- How will difficulties be brought up and dealt with, such as group dynamics, misuse of power, standards of practice?
- Management of tendencies to use the group for personal therapy
- How will good practice be noted or celebrated?

The type of facilitation most beneficial when talking through client work varies for each person. Some like the cut and thrust of many comments and ideas and can manage the energy in the group. Others need a quieter, more structured space with one facilitator to begin with and other participants contributing ideas at the end of the presentation. Still others may prefer a combination of the two styles, with the facilitator managing the process to ensure a useful outcome.

Marianne was new to the group and realized she was starting to withhold some of her concerns about a client and feeling overwhelmed by the amount of advice from other members. She asked for one person to facilitate her through presenting a client and then for other comments at the end after she had had time to consider what was gained in the first interaction. This allowed Marianne to feel her way into the group process and prompted a subsequent general discussion about varying their approach.

For Reflection

If you are familiar with group supervision:

■ How do you choose what and how you present?
■ What type of facilitation suits your way of thinking and understanding?

Group dynamics

The need for members of supervision groups to have theoretical knowledge of group dynamics may or may not be apposite when experiencing undercurrents affecting the comfort or functioning of the group.

Tuckman (1965) uses forming, storming, norming, performing to capture the progress of a group from beginning to a fully functioning organism. Bion (1961), meanwhile, postulates certain characteristics of group behaviours such as dependency, withdrawal due to feeling intimidated by more assertive members, and pairing off or creating subgroups. Both pairing and splitting can occur in the group, as can hiding or letting others do the work. Schultz (1989) talks about the inclusion and belonging needs of an individual and how these affect group dynamics. Supervisees may find it helpful to consider their response to groups and notice their choice of 'should I be in or out?' behaviours.

Understanding one's own contributions to the dynamics within the supervision group plays an important part in assisting the group to work through difficulties and perform effectively for its members.

Building, repairing and maintaining a supervision group alliance

As in many other professional situations, preparation is a key element in ensuring that one's own needs and those of the group are equally met. Boxes 8.2 and 8.3 offer prompts for reflection on your responses and contribution.

For Reflection

Own development

■ Notice your own behaviour in groups and be aware of any tendency to hold back either in asking for time or in censoring what you bring into the group. Does this reflect a natural defence or does the group feel unsafe?
■ Notice methods of presenting that work well for you. What time do you take in the group for your own supervision needs? Do you ever help others get their needs met at the expense of your clients and yourself?

For Reflection

Group cohesion and development

- Notice and take advantage of the strengths of other members. Is one person good at hearing relationship dynamics and does s/he therefore take responsibility for group cohesion?
- Do you have concerns about the group's ways of working? These could include:
  - unhelpful behaviours on the part of some members
  - methods of facilitation that are unproductive: for example, if everyone chimes in, it can be hard to hear important points or to know which are more apposite.
- How might you bring these concerns to the group's awareness?
- If you are still dissatisfied with the group or facilitator, what opportunities are there for confronting this or changing to another group?

The combination of processes in which counsellors each bring clients, issues and dynamics can make the group a confusing place to be. Added to this are sometimes challenging dynamics, evidenced for example by:

- competition for time and support
- need for attention from or status in the group
- 'difficult' members, such as those demanding a disproportionate level of attention or using group time for personal issues (Goldberg, 1981).

> Graham felt angry that Maslam was talking a lot in the group. Everyone seemed to listen intently and even the facilitator did not intervene. Graham was envious of the attention Maslam was receiving and wanted the facilitator to take control and give clear direction. He avoided speaking up, remained dissatisfied and lost an opportunity for himself and others to work through an important phase in developing the group dynamics.

There may be the risk of different factions developing in a group, bringing a potential for bullying and exclusion if relationship complexities are left unattended. Effective supervision groups are open and willing to reflect on their own processes. When they are ineffective, they can be defensive and unskilled at managing difficulties.

Gail had said on more than one occasion that she had met a client over coffee in a local cafe. Clive had questioned her reason for that decision the first time, to which Gail had responded by getting upset and accused him of being authoritarian. He felt unable to pick it up again in the group. Roger was also concerned about the same behaviour but was reluctant to challenge Gail as one of his own development needs had been identified as maintenance of boundaries in therapeutic relationships. Because Gail's responses were not explored or challenged by members, the group colluded with her apparently unethical behaviour. The need to avoid further distress in Gail and in the group overrode ethical responsibilities.

For Reflection

■ How might you face a similar ethical issue in your group?
■ If you are not heard, what might be a next step?

When a group member has the courage and determination to make the first move in raising an issue, and to hold that challenge until it is heeded, the group has the opportunity to look at its processes and to change. If the group cannot accept such a challenge, the quality of supervision is affected, ethical principles may be neglected and the group becomes less of a place of learning, support and safety. This 'storming' phase has a critical role in identifying problems for the group to address. They can then be worked with to provide a healthy and stimulating environment (Tuckman & Jensen, 1977).

It is not unusual for groups to concentrate on one area of work that suits the style of the facilitator or group members. Some groups may find them-selves emphasizing support of members at the expense of challenging poor practice and ethical standards, or entirely focusing on the minutiae of client pathology, with group maintenance and repair bearing the cost. Whatever the preferred model of activity, the task of attending to the group should never be assumed to look after itself for too long.

Peer group supervision

Created by their members, peer supervision groups are well placed to provide equality and commitment from the outset. Organizational demands may not be as dominant as in work-based groups but members have the same supervision tasks and similar professional, ethical and legal considerations to encompass, including monitoring standards and group dynamics. The opportunity to exchange ideas and experiences is consistent with any group situation. At the same time, there are the usual complexities of managing participant interaction, the balance of power in the group and ensuring that the focus is held.

Peer pairs or co-supervision

Two practitioners entering a peer supervision relationship are usually experienced counsellors, often at a similar stage of development. They may share a theoretical approach, and a wish to work in a more collegial climate than in one where there is a possible imbalance in the supervisor/supervisee relationship. The individuals take turns to be supervisor and supervisee and share time equally, sometimes within one session or in alternate sessions.

However experienced the counsellors, co-supervision is an intensive experience. Similar issues arise as with any supervisory relationship: the importance of agreement about ways of working, managing ethical and legal aspects and discussion of the relationship as it contributes to or negatively affects the learning of either person. Competition is not unknown in co-supervision and neither is the difficulty of challenging such a close ally. Boundary issues may be more complex because of possible social and professional connections and relationships.

This is an inexpensive way to ensure regular and efficient supervision and can be engaged in alongside other modes if the caseload demands it, or to gain a wider experience in an open and supportive environment.

TELEPHONE SUPERVISION

Background

Telephone counselling has formed a part of the provision of therapeutic services for some considerable time. Employee assistance programmes regularly offer phone interventions either for crisis intervention or for short-term counselling, and telephone contact and debriefs can form part of their service to counsellors. For some therapists, phone supervision is primarily a 'stop gap' or emergency intervention as in cases of:

- travel difficulties in extreme weather conditions
- supervisee recovering from injury or illness
- an additional session agreed between counsellor and supervisor within their contract to deal with urgent concerns.

In these situations the supervisory relationship and processes have been established and communication through the medium of the telephone should be straightforward.

For practitioners who offer telephone counselling, telephone supervision is a necessary and important companion to their day-to-day activity and provides a comparable experience to that of their clients. If both parties are already experienced in face to face supervision they can adapt their way of working to be just as effective over the phone. For some it takes time to develop the relationship and approach. In the absence of non-verbal cues, the level of concentration on the auditory input is inevitably high.

Contracting for supervision will attend to the same factors as for face to face meetings, but with the additional inclusion of ethical and practical aspects specific to use of the telephone.

Considerations when choosing telephone supervision

The theory of perceptual channels suggests that each person has a favoured mode of taking in information: visual, kinaesthetic or auditory. If you do not naturally tend to the last of these three, it may take time for you to adjust to using it effectively as the sole source of input. Equally, if you have a physical impairment which reduces the viability of the medium, this needs to be borne in mind. The pros and cons of this option are summarized in Table 8.2.

Preparing for and presenting in telephone supervision sessions

Supervision accessed by telephone requires attention to certain practical details. Typically, it is important to have checked out:

- the room used and its comfort
- confidentiality: being aware of the travel of sound in and out of the room and ensuring interruptions are avoided
- (if using a cordless or mobile phone) adequate battery level for the duration of the call
- everything you are likely to need is to hand: notes, pen and paper, diary for future appointment, glass of water.

Attention to emotional and physical reactions during the call helps the supervisee to maintain contact with the supervisor and the issues being discussed. As with any supervision, thought given to the issues in advance will increase the effectiveness of the call, and reflection afterwards will assist in integrating outcomes into practice.

Table 8.2 Advantages and limitations of supervision by telephone

Advantages	Limitations
• Choice of supervisor from a wider geographical area • Greater selection of supervisors with specialist subject knowledge or experienced in telephone counselling and supervision • No need to be physically mobile • Not having to allow time for travel to and from supervision • Ecologically more efficient • Less distraction from non-verbal and other visual input • Enables focused concentration and can access depth more easily through attention to tone, pitch, pace, hesitancy and other paralinguistic signals • The apparent anonymity of not being face to face can bring more openness and may help the supervisee to feel at ease • Thoughtfulness about use of words can bring accuracy in reflection and challenge • Increased use of concentration and listening skills in both parties	• Difficulty accessing a supervisor experienced in telephone work • No access to visual cues to emotions or physical reactions of the other person • Requires an ability to develop relationships through the medium of telephone. Some people fare better in face to face interactions • Demands good hearing as a telephone can distort some sounds and background noise can be distracting • The level of concentration required and frequent checking out of understanding can be tiring • Important non-verbal communication is missing • Time is needed to get used to voice tones, accents, patterns of speech, impressions of the other person and their context • Because body language is not available, care needs to be taken that supervision does not get embroiled in supposition or fantasy about the client or each other

SUPERVISION VIA SKYPE

Online communication tools such as skype have become increasingly popular in recent times, providing an alternative and economical form of accessing supervision. Having similarities to both telephone and online methods, skype sits between the two, enabling two or more people, each with access to a PC, to communicate via:

■ webcam (so that the other person/s can be seen)
■ audio link (working in much the same way as the telephone) or
■ text messaging system (similar to MSN and other text-based online communication tools).

What follows deals primarily with the audio and visual elements of skype supervision. Both this section and the following online supervision section have been informed by the BACP's *Guidelines for Online Counselling and Psychotherapy* (2009).

Counsellors and supervisors might opt to use skype for supervision for much the same reasons as those already outlined for telephone supervision. However, skype has the added benefit of being a free facility, which is especially advantageous when there is a significant geographical distance between the counsellor and supervisor. Skype may also provide an alternative when there are harsh weather conditions and travel is limited. In addition, skype allows the counsellor and supervisor to see each other through video link and so some of the visual elements of the process may be present during the dialogue – although there are limitations as often the image is blurred or delayed, so that picking up the detail of facial expression and other visual cues is not always possible.

Suitability

If skype is the only means of accessing supervision, the supervisee needs to choose a supervisor who not only meets their practice needs, but who can also deliver supervision effectively in this way. Contracting might need to include verification of qualifications and professional registration of both parties, unless the two people are already familiar with one another. An existing supervisory relationship is likely to be a real benefit to getting things started. If either the supervisee or supervisor (or both) have no experience of using skype, then the process may be hindered or overshadowed by the technical learning taking place. Training in and experience with using skype is certainly an advantage.

Supervision via skype is not for everyone. Some may experience the physical distance disconcerting, affecting the level of trust or authenticity in the relationship. Others may feel that this frees them up to be more open in the relationship. Any echo experienced on the line may be distracting and impact on the ability to pick up tone of voice and other verbal cues. If you have already used skype for personal use, it would be worth reflecting on your experience and on how this might translate into supervision prior to starting a supervisory relationship using this medium.

Confidentiality

It is particularly important to consider how confidentiality might be compromised before using skype for supervision. There is a risk that conversations could be intercepted, particularly if supervision is taking place on an unsecure network or within an organization where an IT department has full system access. To ensure the confidentiality of supervision sessions using skype:

- Use a computer that is encrypted and accesses the internet via a network that is both secure and private.
- Carefully consider the location where skype sessions will take place to ensure you can't be overheard. The use of headphones will also help to reduce the risks.
- The names of clients or any other distinctive identifying material should not be used during supervision sessions.

Ethical, professional and legal requirements

As with all supervision arrangements, contracting should include all relevant information about when and how any disclosures are to be made and how concerns about practice will be communicated. Clarity is especially important when there is a geographical distance between the supervisor and supervisee so that any significant differences in requirements, policy or procedures are highlighted. If supervision is taking place across national boundaries, both parties need to be aware of any differences in professional or legal requirements that may apply to both the supervision and the counselling practice.

Technical difficulties

Skype is not always a reliable form of communication. Often an echo or delay can be experienced on the line which may impact negatively on the flow of sessions and the clarity of interaction. If communication during a session is poor, the quality of the interaction may be enhanced if the video call is dropped and an audio call is used on its own. Any interruptions to the internet service or a computer malfunction may abruptly force an ending to a session in mid-flow. If the supervisor and supervisee are in different countries or in remote areas, there may be a greater risk of internet unreliability, particularly if one person is living in an area that does not have access to more up-to-date internet services. Agreeing beforehand how such difficulties will be managed should include:

- if supervision can resume via another method such as the telephone
- a time limit to wait whilst attempting to rectify any interruption to service
- when and how sessions will be rescheduled.

Cultural differences

There may be significant differences in the cultural norms of counselling if the supervisee is practising in a different country to that of the supervisor. In these circumstances it is important that the supervisee ensures that the supervisor fully understands any differences and takes these into consideration during supervision.

> Georgina is the only counsellor on a remote island and accesses supervision via skype. The island has a small community where nearly everyone is known to each other. Georgina is often in counselling relationships with clients whom she has contact with in other settings, who know each other or who are known to Georgina's family. Dual and multiple relationships are commonplace and supervision often focuses on the difficulties of managing these relationships and preserving the therapeutic alliance and space. It took time for her supervisor to fully understand the complexity of these relationships and to adapt to the uniqueness of Georgina's practice.

ONLINE SUPERVISION

The world of the internet and computers is a fast changing technological landscape and it is important to acknowledge any developments that may have occurred since the time of writing. Events surrounding the media scandal (in 2011/12) in the UK highlighted the ability of the law to access deleted e-mails. Reports of computer hackers are common. Changes to the law are proposed regarding rights to privacy, and there are moves to extend government access to internet communication in the light of increasing external threats from terrorism. Even younger people – usually the most relaxed about the internet and social networking sites – are joining in the growing public anxiety about the degree of privacy afforded when using these media as communication tools.

Despite all of this, online counselling and psychotherapy is growing in popularity, together with provision of online supervision by e-mail or using real time, text-based messaging systems. Provided any potential compromise to confidentiality is addressed, online supervision can be invaluable for some practitioners. This option may well be a viable solution if location and ease of access to suitable face to face supervision is problematic. A counsellor who is practising online therapy may seek online supervision to mirror and support the medium by which counselling is being provided. For some, particularly kinaesthetic learners, using the written form may be a benefit to reflexivity and the supervision process. In these circumstances, choosing online supervision might be the only or the most appropriate means of receiving supervision. Table 8.3 sets out the pros and cons of this medium.

Table 8.3 Strengths and limitations of online supervision

Strengths	Limitations
• Beneficial for online counsellors: supports and mirrors therapeutic practice • Alternative source when access to supervision is limited • If using e-mail, can allow time for reflection in between interactions, leading to more considered responses • Increased choice of provision, such as easier access to supervisor with specialist experience or reduced risk of dual or multiple relationships • The depth of the work may be increased for some if there is a sense of remoteness or anonymity • On-going written record of supervision process allowing for reflection on the detail of previous sessions	• Requires additional training and practice experience: some practitioners are not familiar with communicating in this way • Technical difficulties can interrupt the process • Gaps between responses may interrupt the flow and limit the quality of the process • Absence of visual and verbal cues may lead to important elements being missed or confusion of meaning • Editing of detail may more easily occur leading to important elements being omitted (either unintentionally or intentionally) thus limiting the depth of process or relationship • Increased risk of accidental breaches to confidentiality

Online options

The medium through which supervision will be conducted needs to be agreed explicitly at the outset. The most popular methods include e-mail used asynchronously, which may be most useful for those living in different time zones, or text-based instant messaging systems (such as MSN) which allow for real time 'virtual' conversations to take place. Any synchronistic supervision arrangement needs to consider, during the contracting stage, the potential for interruptions to sessions as a result of technical difficulties. There should be agreement on how problems of this kind will be managed. If using e-mail, the supervisor and supervisee must be clear about their expectations of the other, such as how long each will wait for a response from the other. Some supervisory pairs choose to use a combination of e-mail and text-based messaging systems. An e-mail outlining a supervision issue might be sent to the supervisor prior to a scheduled supervision session, and could then form the focus of the session. For example:

> Hello, Grace. I've been thinking about our last supervision discussion and would like next time for us to further explore my work with my male client 'B'. I had a session with him yesterday and he was contradicting everything that I said, as if he wanted a fight with me rather than a counselling session. I attempted to revisit his goals for counselling but I was so exasperated by this point, I know that it showed. I am left feeling tired and confused and not sure what is going on or where to go with him. I would welcome any initial thoughts you may have when we speak on Thursday. Thanks, Caitlin.

Contracting

Contracts for online supervision require the same careful consideration and negotiation as for face to face meetings. In addition and aside from agreeing the online communication tool, there are specific elements of online supervision to address at the outset:

- **Scheduling of sessions and availability for contact:** Duration; frequency; emergency supervision arrangements; time frame between asynchronous communications; protocol for contact outside scheduled slots and respecting boundaries in this regard; methods of communicating availability.
- **Management of technical difficulties:** Agree a strategy to adopt when the chosen technology proves troublesome.
- **Record keeping:** Written modes of online communication provide an automatic record of the content of supervision sessions. Supervisor and supervisee need to agree on whether one or both will keep these records and for how long, when and how they will be disposed of and who might have access to them.
- **Legal requirements:** Supervisor and supervisee should be aware of and adhere to data protection law and may consider becoming registered as keepers of sensitive information. Knowledge of legal requirements when practising in different countries is essential: there may be differences in the law regarding the communication and storage of sensitive information, legislation pertaining to issues of risk and regarding disclosure.

- **Confidentiality:** An agreement needs to be established on how best to preserve the confidentiality of supervision and therapeutic processes to protect clients (see below).

Confidentiality and security

The confidentiality of supervision is the most important aspect to be considered before starting an online supervision arrangement. The names of clients and other identifiable material should not be shared in online supervision. Informed consent of clients should be obtained before text from any written communication which has formed part of the therapeutic process is shared in supervision or elsewhere. The same principle applies to supervision in that no part of the actual text from the online dialogue should be shared elsewhere (e.g. by the supervisor in supervision of supervision) without the prior consent of the supervisee – unless there is a specific ethical or legal reason for doing so.

It is advisable that the computer used should be in a protected location so that others cannot overlook and read any of the written text. Access to the internet should be secure and private and the use of passwords and encryption is essential to achieve maximum security of information being shared. Although having these systems in place will provide some peace of mind, they still cannot offer a complete guarantee of security. Any inadvertent breaches of confidentiality, such as accidentally forwarding an e-mail to another person, will need to be communicated immediately to the relevant parties unless, for instance in the case of a particularly vulnerable client, it is considered harmful to do so. Any decisions to withhold information about confidentiality breaches must be professionally, ethically and legally justified.

Keeping up to date

As stated above, the world of technology is forever changing, as are the means of manipulating and intercepting internet systems for criminal activity. It is therefore important that supervisor and supervisee keep abreast of developments, research and changes to the law. It is advisable that both have undergone training in online supervision or counselling and engage in regular, relevant CPD activities to keep abreast of professional guidelines. Joining a peer support forum for online counsellors is also worth considering so that good practice can be shared.

CREATIVITY IN SUPERVISION

The final part of this chapter explores options for diversifying and enhancing supervision, resting on the premise that many counsellors would benefit from increasing their use of creative approaches in the supervision space as a means to gain inspiration and insight and to uncover unconscious processes. Employing these strategies in supervision can also enable counsellors to practise their application, thus enhancing integration into therapeutic practice. Examples include:

- use of imagery and metaphor
- guided fantasy/visualization
- therapeutic picture cards
- small objects (e.g. figures, toys, animals, bricks, buttons, pebbles)
- drawing and art work
- role play/imagined dialogues
- letter writing
- creating narratives or stories
- reflective writing/journaling
- music
- psychodrama
- sand-tray
- diagrams
- (specifically for groups): sculpting and 'fishbowl' (see Proctor, 2008).

Right or left brain?

In addition to the introduction to learning styles provided in Chapter 3, it is worthwhile considering the concept developed by Sperry (1980) in which the left and right sides of the brain are said to process information differently (Table 8.4). The theory suggests that one side is often dominant, with a consequent impact on the person's ability to engage in creative activities.

This theory has more recently been expanded upon. Current thinking is that when both sides of the brain are being accessed, cognitive and learning processes are more effective (Singh & Boyle, 2004). Working creatively can bring about an integration of both sides of the brain, bringing new ideas into awareness (Lahad, 2002; Shuck & Wood, 2011).

A supervisee who predominately uses the left side of the brain may find it more difficult to engage with creative approaches so it can be helpful to prepare the brain for working in a different way. This could be through free-association writing or drawing, meditation, going for a walk or listening to music – whatever works best for you.

Table 8.4   Left and right brain functions

Left brain	Right brain
Rational thought processes	Taps into emotions and feelings easily – has emotional literacy
Uses logic to work out problems – linear and sequential patterns of thinking	Intuitive
Analytical mind – good at mathematical processes	Is naturally imaginative and creative
Verbal	Visual
Tends to look at the finer details first before putting them together to get the whole picture	Tends to look holistically at the whole picture before the finer detail

---

For Reflection

Understanding blocks, reluctance or resistance

- How do you feel about using creative techniques?
- Do you usually engage with creative practices freely or do you experience some discomfort?
- If so, can you:
  - Name your discomfort?
  - Identify where it comes from, e.g. does it remind you of a past situation?
- Is there a way of addressing any discomfort – perhaps some way of rationalizing it?
- If the discomfort belongs to the 'here and now', how could this be resolved?
- Could your supervisor help you with this in the supervision process?

Making use of creative strategies in supervision

The range of creative strategies listed earlier provides a set of effective tools to describe clients, their context and the therapeutic relationship; to reveal unconscious thoughts, feelings and processes; and to evoke aspects of the supervision space. Lahad (2002) and Proctor (2008) are among the authors included in the recommended reading list at the end of this chapter who offer ways by which creativity can be developed in supervision. Additionally, Chapter 6 provides examples of how creative writing can be utilized to access your internal supervisor and to work with the impact of a sudden, unplanned ending of a supervisory relationship. It is worth noting that there are no fixed rules about how any of these strategies should be used: accessing your creative energies means being free from the constraints of a 'technique' and going with the flow of what comes. To get the best out of any creative approach:

- Be sure that you are in the right frame of mind and tell your supervisor if you are not.
- Make sure that you understand what the purpose of the task is and what it involves before starting.
- Let go of any ideas about getting it right or wrong – remember, there are no fixed rules.
- Remember that this is not an art class or something similar– you are not going to be judged on your creative abilities.
- Allow time to debrief the activity at the end.
- Make a note of and bring back any thoughts or feelings that emerge after supervision has ended – it is common for processing to continue beyond the session.

1. Therapeutic picture cards

A number of companies have produced picture cards specifically designed for use as therapeutic tools, although a good collection of picture postcards can be just as effective. They can be used in a variety of different ways in both therapy and supervision. The cards used in the example (Figure 8.1) are produced by OH-Publishing.

> Gillian was feeling stuck with her client and experiencing a sense of inadequacy. After some discussion she was still unable to pinpoint where these feelings were coming from. Damon, her supervisor, suggested that she used the picture cards to describe what is going on in the therapeutic relationship. In silence, Gillian carefully chose the cards that she felt drawn to and then placed them in the format below. Damon then helped Gillian to describe each card, enabling her to tap into the thoughts and feelings that each evoked and what this might tell her about the client and their relationship.

The client often presented as a small boy, much younger than his years and emotionally cut off from Gillian and others. Gillian was struggling to find a way to enable him to access his feelings.

The client had anger issues and this was at times projected onto Gillian. The client seemed to want her to 'back off' as soon as she went close to his emotions and she was often left with a feeling of not being good enough for him.

Gillian experienced the client as being in turbulent water. She felt reluctant to enter the storm, being scared of 'drowning' with him. She realized that she had sub-consciously avoided areas of emotional difficulty.

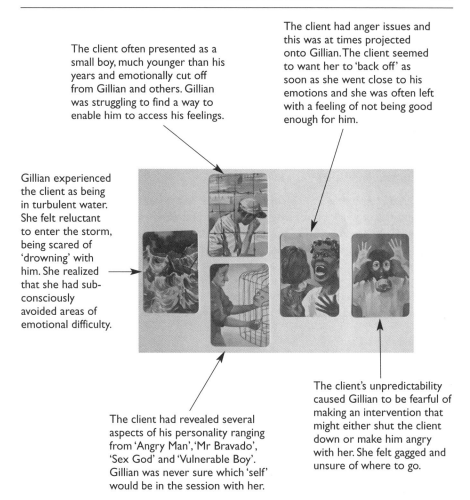

The client had revealed several aspects of his personality ranging from 'Angry Man', 'Mr Bravado', 'Sex God' and 'Vulnerable Boy'. Gillian was never sure which 'self' would be in the session with her.

The client's unpredictability caused Gillian to be fearful of making an intervention that might either shut the client down or make him angry with her. She felt gagged and unsure of where to go.

Figure 8.1   Using therapeutic picture cards

By exploring her feelings towards the client and the work, Gillian was able to achieve a better understanding of what was really going on. She hadn't realized until now the extent of the client's vulnerability, which was being kept well hidden behind his anger and bravado. Supervision helped her re-ground and tap back into inner resources of strength and patience that were needed to sit with the client and earn his trust.

2. Using small objects

A good collection of figures, small toys, animals, bricks, buttons or pebbles is an essential component of the creative practitioner's tool kit. Small objects are incredibly versatile resources, providing a wide range of different uses in both counselling and supervision.

> Ray's client has a complex family background. Both he and his supervisor, Ken, were struggling to make sense of and hold on to the client's context in relation to significant others.
>
> Firstly, Ken asked Ray to choose a button that represented the client and then to pick buttons that he felt characterized the client's friends and family members. Ray positioned these buttons to symbolize where he felt they might be in relation to the client. The exercise not only helped Ray and Ken to get a better sense of who's who in the client's life, but also raised awareness of the different characters in the story, the relational dynamics at play as well as some gaps in Ray's own understanding of the client's context (Figure 8.2).

Grandparents from the client's father's side. Relationship breakdown with the mother gets in the way of the client's relationship with them.

The client.

Client's aunt and uncle, situated at some distance.

The client's father, step-mother and step-sister. These are positioned in the background as the client has little contact with them. The client's father is portrayed by their mother as a 'bad man'.

The client's mother and step-family. The mother is situated in closer proximity to the client as if shielding them from the others, with whom the client does not have a good relationship.

The client's younger half-sister.

Client's friends are situated nearest to the client.

Grandparents from the client's mother's side.

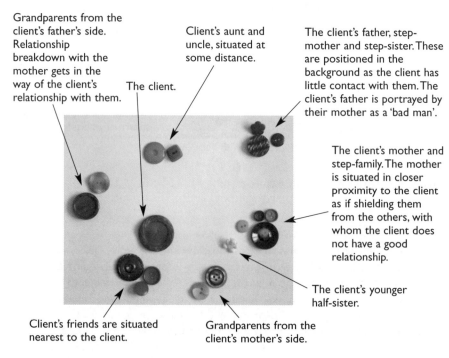

Figure 8.2   Using small objects

3. *Role play*

Role play can be used in a number of ways in supervision. It can be a particularly useful strategy for enacting dialogues with a view to gaining clarity about how the counsellor might approach a situation or to shed light on complex relational dynamics. The role play might involve using an empty chair for the absent person, with the counsellor speaking to the 'other' and then imagining how they might respond. Alternatively, it could involve the supervisor taking on the role of either the counsellor or the other person in an interaction. These could include:

- potential counsellor–client dialogues such as managing a difficult ending with a client
- possible dialogues between the counsellor and other professionals, as in a dispute with a manager.

Supervision accessed in a group setting can include productive use of role play, 'fishbowl' and sculpting activities (Proctor, 2008), taking advantage of the opportunity afforded by having a number of people to represent the protagonists.

4. *Using reflective writing to benefit supervision*

Most counsellors have kept a reflective journal at some stage of their development, usually during training. It can be useful to continue with some form of reflective writing beyond the training stage to further develop reflexivity by exploring personal and professional issues and themes. Engaging with reflective writing before or after supervision sessions can enhance awareness of the self as practitioner. It can also help to increase the depth of engagement in supervision by keeping track of developmental themes and provide an opportunity to reflect on the supervisory relationship. It is best to be spontaneous and uncensored in writing to allow thoughts and expression to flow freely and to see what emerges. Taking extracts of reflective writing to supervision may also be beneficial to support further exploration of emerging themes.

Achieving the right degree of creativity in supervision

The level of creativity in supervision inevitably depends to some extent on the supervisor's style as well as on other influences such as organizational requirements that dictate the focus and content of sessions. The supervisor's approach may be naturally creative. It may, in contrast, be more verbal and analytical. To help achieve the right balance of creativity, ask yourself:

■ Am I comfortable with the degree of creativity in evidence in my supervision sessions?
■ Does this fit with my learning and communication style?
■ How might an increase in my level of creativity benefit me and my practice?
■ If creativity is lacking, how might I work with my supervisor to make this happen?

IN SUMMARY

It may be important from time to time to review the structure, medium or style of supervision and to incorporate other options into the counsellor's repertoire. Favoured alternatives to the supervision dyad include group and peer formats. When considering group supervision, there are potential benefits from the input of numbers of fellow practitioners. The choice of group is important, as are the details of the contract. The therapist may need to experiment with different modes of presenting and it can take time to collaborate with peers to establish an effective group process. Whatever configuration is adopted, the functional role of guardianship of professional standards must be securely in place.

Both established and newer technologies present other possibilities to deal with practical hurdles or the specifics of individual requirements. Phone, skype and internet-based methodologies all offer a range of practical advantages, especially to those in remoter locations or prevented from easy access to face to face supervision. The concerns to be addressed relate particularly to confidentiality and data security – as well as to the need for strategies to circumvent technical problems when they arise.

Extending the counsellor's range in supervision can involve developing the use of creative strategies within the familiar dyadic structure. Having a resource of materials can support the adoption of innovative activity. It may need to be the supervisee who prompts a level of experimentation in order to gain the new understandings these approaches can reveal.

Recommended reading

BACP (2009) *Guidelines for Online Counselling and Psychotherapy*, 3rd edn (Lutterworth: BACP).

Carroll, M. (2004) 'Forms of Supervision and Presentation in Supervision' (Chapter 7), *Counselling Supervision: Theory, Skills and Practice* (London: Sage), pp. 129–147.

Goss, S. (2000) 'A Supervisory Revolution? The Impact of New Technology' in Lawson, B. & Feltham, C. (eds) *Taking Supervision Forward: Enquiries and Trends in Counselling and Psychotherapy* (London: Sage), pp. 175–189.

Jones, G. & Stokes, A. (2009) *Online Counselling: A Handbook for Practitioners* (Basingstoke: Palgrave Macmillan).

Lago, C. & Wright, J. (2007) 'E-mail Supervision' in Tudor, K. & Worrall, M. (eds) *Freedom to Practise Volume II: Developing Person-Centred Approaches to Supervision* (Ross-on-Wye: PCCS Books), pp. 102–118.

Lahad, M. (2002) *Creative Supervision: The Use of Expressive Arts Methods in Supervision and Self-Supervision* (London: Jessica Kingsley Publishers).

Proctor, B. (2008) *Group Supervision: A Creative Guide to Supervision*, 2nd edn (London: Sage).

Tuckman, B. & Jensen, M. (1977) 'Stages of Small Group Development Revisited' *Group and Organisational Studies*, 2, 419–427.

Tudor, K. (2007) 'Group Supervision' in Tudor, K. & Worrall, M. (eds) *Freedom to Practise Volume II: Developing Person-Centred Approaches to Supervision* (Ross-on-Wye: PCCS Books), pp. 85–101.

Chapter 9

Ethics in Supervision

INTRODUCTION

Ethics thread through every part of a counsellor's work, its strands reaching influentially into the supervision space. Whilst ethical responsibility was discussed in Chapter 4, this chapter explores how predicaments in the therapy might be addressed in supervision by investigating three case studies for their ethical dimensions. Supervisee and supervisor can work collaboratively to define the ethical issues involved in such situations so as to resource decisions about how they can be effectively managed.

Ethics have been defined as the moral principles that govern a person's behaviour or how an activity is conducted. A dilemma in professional practice is likely to prompt questions about the best course of action in what will always be a unique set of circumstances. The process of weighing up the most appropriate way forward can be complex, with a number of elements influencing thinking – including theory and codes, personal and professional morality and values (Carroll, 2004).

A number of ethical codes and frameworks have been published by the governing bodies for psychological therapies in the UK, all with the aim of providing their members with a definition of the principles to which they have subscribed, and focusing on appropriate conduct in relation to clients and the profession as a whole. The main difference between these articulations appears to lie in the use of language. In what follows, the terms of the BACP Ethical Framework (2010) are used as the point of reference.

Ethical decision-making can be fraught with tension and difficulty, particularly when the principles involved clash with each other or with the counsellor's personal beliefs. This can be made even more complex if, after consultation with others, a number of conflicting perspectives emerge. BACP acknowledges that individual practitioners might arrive at diverse outcomes and yet all could be equally justified (BACP, 2010). Thrown into this delicate balancing act are often conflicting pressures of organizational priorities and demands. Supervision provides a space to explore dilemmas to ensure that informed thinking reflects what is best for clients. This enables the counsellor to act with integrity and to feel as confident as possible that they can give account to themselves and others for the decisions taken.

ETHICS IN SUPERVISION: CLIENT PRACTICE ISSUES

Paul came to see Sally for counselling to work on his anger. After 12 sessions the work has being going well. During the 13th session, Paul discloses that he has had an argument with his wife resulting in him lashing out physically. He is feeling shame and remorse about this and admits to Sally that this is not the first time something similar has happened.

Sally had previously decided that working with the perpetrators of domestic violence is outside her competency. Her decision is partly based on experiences during her formative years but also on a belief that she would be unable to offer the core conditions. This position has been intended to ensure that the client group would have a greater chance of accessing alternative and more effective counselling.

Sally's immediate reaction to the disclosure is one of panic and fear. Her urge is to run away and end the counselling work immediately. At the same time, she is also aware of the therapeutic relationship that she has with Paul and is confused by her conflicting feelings. In supervision, the ethical principles listed in Table 9.1 were discussed and weighed up against each other:

Table 9.1   Discussion around ethical principles

Fidelity (being trustworthy):   The trust that Paul has in Sally is evident. If Sally were to end counselling now, Paul might perceive this as a rejection, exacerbating his shame. It would interrupt the therapeutic process, could prevent him from overcoming his issues and hence indirectly risk perpetuating the violence. He may never again find the courage to trust anybody with this sensitive personal material and his anger may stay unresolved.

On the other hand, can Sally maintain her trustworthiness and continue to offer the core conditions? Sally is now party to information that Paul is physically harming his wife. She needs to assess the significance of this and the responsibility this knowledge brings.

Autonomy: Paul has engaged in counselling and the therapeutic relationship is well established. He clearly made this disclosure because he is comfortable with Sally and feels that she is the right person to help him work through this. She wishes to respect his 'right to be self-governing' (BACP, 2010, p. 3). On the flip side, Sally feels really uncomfortable and is unsure if she can continue. She is no longer sure if she is the right counsellor for Paul.

Sally also needs to consider her own autonomy and right to choose whether and when she can work with clients or needs to refer on.   ⏵

Table 9.1 (continued)

Beneficence (promoting client well-being): Exploring this aspect demonstrates Sally's 'commitment to acting in the best interests of the client' (BACP, 2010, p. 3). Sally is concerned that she may impact negatively on this client if she continues to work with him – but she is equally worried about the negative impact of referring him on. The pros and cons of each are discussed at length. Whilst wanting to respect Paul's autonomy, Sally is not convinced that his decision to work with her is fully informed. If she shares her difficulty with Paul, whether or not they continue to work together, he may well see this as a judgement. Whilst considering the possibility of continuing counselling, CPD training options and various reading materials are explored.

Non-maleficence (doing no harm): Sally is concerned that her personal history may get in the way of offering Paul unconditional positive regard or fail to encourage him to be open about his experiences. Her need to privilege her own self-protection could diminish her competency in the work. Personal therapy is discussed as an option for Sally so that if she continues in the counselling work, she has a space where she can bracket off her own material.

Justice (fairness): Sally also contemplates her obligation to treat all clients equally and that if she ended with the client now it could be viewed as discriminatory. In contrast, she is concerned that by continuing to work with him, she may be favouring Paul over other clients whom she has refused to work with in the past.

Likewise, any diminution of Sally's ability to offer the core conditions to this client would not be providing him with a fair service.

Self-respect (practitioner self-care): Sally's decision not to work with perpetrators of domestic violence was not only in the spirit of doing what is right for the client, but also to protect herself from the re-emergence of difficult past memories due to potential triggers in the therapeutic work.

In addition to CPD activities and the possibility of personal counselling if she is to continue working with Paul, Sally thinks about other ways she could look after herself. These include giving herself plenty of time before and after sessions to prepare and re-ground herself, as well as considering additional supervision. Risk and safety issues are also thought through and possible strategies are discussed.

> After detailed discussion with her supervisor, Sally is aware that despite her initial reaction to Paul's disclosure, she still has considerable respect and empathy for him. She has witnessed Paul's vulnerability and can see that he is a desperate man who is very keen to work through his problems and resolve them. She recognizes that, whilst it is challenging to continue, it does not mean that she will lose herself or her values. By putting the right strategies in place, such as personal counselling and additional supervision, she can be facilitated and supported to take care of both herself and the client. She is also helped to see that this work has the potential to help her overcome a sticking point in her practice and further her development in a way she never thought possible before.

It is important in this situation to carefully assess one's competence and personal resilience alongside other factors relating to personal safety and the ability to offer best practice. Much of this will depend on the individual counsellor, the client, the context and the support systems already in place or that could be put in place. Supervision can offer a third person perspective and enable a thorough exploration of the influencing elements. These might include some or all of the following:

Counsellor:

- Individual beliefs and values
- Past and current circumstances
- Developmental stage
- Experience of working with certain problems
- Current caseload and intensity of client work as a whole
- Support systems (professional and personal)
- Self-care strategies.

Client:

- Nature of the issues and degree of complexity
- Potential risk factors to self or others.

Organizational:

- Number of counselling sessions allocated
- Internal and external referral systems
- Organizational requirements in relation to professional practice, organizational policy and the law.

For Reflection

- Are there client groups or issues that you have decided it would be best for you not to work with?
- What would your immediate thoughts and feelings be if you found yourself in a similar position to Sally?
- What factors would you need to consider to ensure that the best course of action is taken?
- Is there anything that you would need to put in place to support your decision?

WORKING WITH AN ORGANIZATIONAL ETHICAL DILEMMA

It is not only the client work that can raise dilemmas for a therapist: organizational settings are another frequent source of concern. For many reasons it is not unusual for a counsellor to feel isolated and pressured in their workplace. The values and principles associated with the therapeutic profession can at times be at odds, or even in direct conflict, with business drivers and objectives. It is a fine line to negotiate a productive way forward without compromising the counsellor's principles, and at the same time avoid being seen as precious or immature.

> Ben is one of a team of staff counsellors working in the Occupational Health Department of his company. Out of the blue he receives an e-mail from his manager Shobana, requesting he does two shifts on reception a week with immediate effect. She goes on to suggest that as it is frequently not busy, he will be able to write up his notes at the same time. Ben is unimpressed by this development and concerned about the ethical implications. He is angry when he arrives at his supervision with Mary.
>
> **Ben:** You won't believe what they've asked me to do now. I'm furious. They want me to do reception in my admin time when I'm supposed to be writing up my notes. This is demeaning and unethical in so many ways. I'll see my clients come and go, have visibility of their attendance, never mind writing my notes in a public place. I feel like just telling Shobana it is not on.
>
> **Mary:** I appreciate you are angry. How can I best support you in this?
>
> **Ben:** I guess I need to let off steam and then think it through more carefully before I decide what to do.
>
> **Mary:** So how about you tell me more about how you are feeling and then maybe it would help to weigh up the ethics of the situation prior to you talking to Shobana.

In the lengthy exchange that ensued the opportunities and problems involved in going along with Shobana's decision were considered. The discussion linked these to the ethical principles at stake:

Table 9.2 Ethical principles – opportunities and problems

Opportunities	Problems
Being trustworthy: The counsellor could remain trustworthy in the clients' eyes if he has an opportunity to meet all his clients to notify and re-contract to minimize surprises. Client notes are not attended to whilst on reception and alternative times will be identified for this.	Clients' notes will be in a public place with a chance of being seen. Clients' expectations that this is a private relationship will be compromised, potentially eroding trust. Existing and future clients may see their counsellor chatting to other staff, which may diminish their belief in the confidentiality of the relationship.
Autonomy: Counsellors need to be seen to fulfil their obligations as an employee.	Clients may feel that their attendance is being checked or monitored by their counsellor (e.g. if they choose to attend work, but not counselling).
Beneficence (promoting well-being): If discussed carefully with clients and appropriate assurances made, it may offer appropriate role modelling of organizational flexibility.	The client may well feel the therapeutic relationship is compromised and be unable to continue.
Non-maleficence (avoiding harm): There is an opportunity to find a compromise such that the service continues to operate ethically in these difficult times.	Other counsellors in the team may be persuaded to blindly follow this new request without reflecting on the impact on their clients.
Justice (fairness): All employees are faced with similar pressures and challenges.	Clients working in this office will be more affected than clients from other premises who visit purely to attend Occupational Health. If other counsellors are offered less public administrative tasks, they and their clients will not be as compromised as Ben.
Self-respect: This is an opportunity for the counsellor to demonstrate resilience and flexibility. It could be a development/career enhancing opportunity.	This seems like poor use of a skilled professional. It feels as if he is being under-valued – like a demotion. The situation puts him under additional pressure.

Ben recognized that he was not going to be viewed in a positive light if he simply insisted that this request was unethical and he was unable to offer any alternative. He was surprised in his dialogue with Mary that ways forward emerged. It no longer felt like a hopeless situation. This allowed him to identify the concerns he was unable to compromise on, specifically his reluctance for client notes to be on reception and a need to meet with all his clients prior to starting his reception duties. It also enabled him to carefully prepare for a meeting with his manager. He felt more confident that he could clearly articulate his worries and make proactive suggestions.

In his following supervision he updated Mary:

> **Ben**: When I met with Shobana she was willing to listen to my worries. She was also able to fill me in on the background. Our company is facing serious financial problems. Throughout the organization budget cuts have been allocated to all managers. The senior management team is committed to employee welfare at this time and has made the decision to avoid making any staff redundant. However, they are keen to reduce their spend on contract workers. Managers have been asked to come up with innovative ways to achieve this. Shobana has decided to let her temporary administrative staff go and intends to share their workload across our team. She recognizes this is far from ideal and that it will bring additional stress to a workforce already under pressure, yet feels she has no choice in the current economic climate.
>
> **Mary**: She and the organization are not being as insensitive as you first thought?
>
> **Ben**: Reluctantly I have to admit not. Actually they are trying to do the best for their staff in a ruthless financial market.
>
> **Mary**: Where does this leave you?
>
> **Ben**: Shobana agreed to rejig the rota so counsellors do not have public administrative tasks such as reception, so no doubt we will be landed with some extremely boring jobs, but won't be compromising our clients.

There is much learning in this scenario. It is easy to jump to conclusions and assume that management teams are behaving unscrupulously, yet the counsellor, whilst honouring personal responses to organizational mandates, can use his finely tuned empathy to gain a broader understanding of the situation. It is rare to find a manager who deliberately seeks to cause harm to others though s/he may well make decisions under pressure that seem disconnected from the consequences and their emotional impact. Managers' aims and measures may well appear to be in direct conflict with those of the therapist, and counsellors can feel buffeted by the forces of change faced by the company. Taking a holistic view and finding out about employers' objectives can be illuminating. Keeping up with organizational drivers and change imperatives, a therapist can work with the grain of the employer's needs in challenging times. It is important to distinguish between demands that can be accommodated and those that cannot, actively seeking effective compromise where this is called for. It is the easy option to resist for the sake of resisting. In the above case the management team had staff welfare high on their agenda and were willing to seek the middle ground.

Having said all that, it is not unusual to hear of businesses putting their staff in extremely difficult situations. Managers under stress, in survival mode, can bulldoze inadequately explained programmes through.

Consider this contrasting scenario:

Mary: How did you get on with Shobana?

Ben: Not well. She didn't want to hear any of it. I feel really worried and bullied, I can't see a way forward.

Mary: Your concerns weren't heard?

Ben: She didn't seem to get it at all. She sees that all the OH staff have confidential patient relationships and we are all in the same boat.

Mary: You sound defeated. Where does that leave you and your clients?

Ben: I feel it is just another instance of poor management and I'm sick of trying to fight my corner for myself and my clients.

Mary: Like an on-going battle.

Ben: Exactly.

Mary: I'm wondering how you are going to look after yourself in this difficult environment and work ethically.

Ben: Well, one thing is for sure. I'm not putting in the extra hours I have been to help clear the waiting list. I'm going to make time for myself.

Mary: And your clients?

Ben: I won't have client notes on reception. I'll have to squeeze in my note-writing somewhere else and I will contact all my clients to alert them that they may see me on reception.

Mary: Sounds like you are prioritizing your clients and withdrawing your goodwill towards the organization.

Ben: Yes, and what worries me more is that some of my colleagues seem to have lost the will to fight and are just going along with whatever they are told.

In order to continue to work ethically with his clients Ben is having to take personal responsibility and commit extra time unsupported by his manager. In these situations it is common for counsellors to feel personally diminished, unable to be heard and faced with a stark choice – collude with a seemingly unethical decision or leave their employment. It is also possible for practitioners, and their in-house supervisors, to get lost in the organizational fog, no longer able to take an objective view of the situation and its moral implications.

ETHICS IN THE SUPERVISORY RELATIONSHIP

How much supervision is ethical?

'All counsellors, psychotherapists…are required to have on-going and formal supervision/consultative support for their work in accordance with professional requirements' (BACP, 2010, p. 6).

The amount of supervision is negotiated between a therapist and their supervisor, although a minimum level of 1.5 hours per month is stipulated by BACP for their accredited practitioners, regardless of caseload. Many practitioners would expect to be receiving more than this minimum in one guise or another. Organizations can be reluctant to contribute financially beyond the base level. Counsellors may need to be creative in accessing additional supervision, for example through peer groups or pairs or by self-financing the shortfall, in the interests of clients and their own well-being.

In considering the appropriate amount of supervision which should be accessed, the following factors come into play:

- volume of clients
- intensity of client work

- range of therapy settings
- supervisee's level of experience
- supervisee's developmental agenda
- personal stressors
- availability of other sources of professional or personal support.

A healthy attitude would ensure that the duration and frequency of any supervision arrangement is regularly reviewed and that a flexible outlook is employed. If a practitioner finds the intensity of their work increases they may increase their supervision for a period and similarly reduce it if the caseload falls away.

Other more emotive factors might be at play. For instance, Rob is employed as a counsellor and his organization pays for 1.5 hours of external independent supervision. He has recently started his own private practice and is discussing his additional supervision requirements with his supervisor.

> **Rob:** Yeah, my private practice is going well. I've got half a dozen clients now and I thought maybe I need some additional supervision.
>
> **Lesley:** You've not been having any supervision for these clients at all?
>
> **Rob:** Well, no. As you know I get 1.5 hours with you through my company and although this is primarily about their clients it indirectly affects my private clients. Much of my learning is transportable.
>
> **Lesley:** I appreciate that. However, your private clients are being overlooked.
>
> **Rob:** Yeah, exactly. That's why I was wondering if I could arrange ad hoc supervision if I feel the need, either tag an extra 30 minutes on to our session or occasionally have an hour focused on them which I'll pay for.
>
> **Lesley:** I'm feeling a little concerned at your reluctance to commit to regular supervision time for these clients now you are paying. They represent over 20 hours a month and maybe warrant regular supervision in their own right. We can always review this as the volume of clients varies. I know how it is in private practice.
>
> **Rob:** I feel I am generally getting more than enough supervision with the 1.5 hours and just wanted to be sure I could access more if I needed to.

This dialogue looks as if it is heading for an impasse. Worryingly, Rob's reluctant attitude points to a lack of commitment to personal and professional growth and to the client safety that supervision can help to provide. For some counsellors the supervisory enterprise is seen more as a box-ticking exercise and its potential benefits are not appreciated. On occasions, given the mandatory demand to participate in supervision, this is understandable, as practitioner autonomy seems to be in doubt. Even with a paucity of client hours, supervision can enable powerful learning. An opportunity to turn the focus away from clients and shine the light more brightly on the supervisee can facilitate deeper self-awareness or provide a forum to debate broader professional topics.

Other indicators of a lacklustre engagement may include regular cancellations, a general lack of enthusiasm or reticence when it comes to entering the sessions wholeheartedly. The lack of motivation a supervisee experiences could arise from a variety of causes, including problems with the supervisor or supervision, or personal issues such as fear of judgement or low self-worth. Various points for reflection suggested in this book are intended to enable the identification of dissatisfaction and promote strategies for resolution.

Supervisory relationship dilemmas

The supervisory dyad is no more immune to uncomfortable predicaments than therapeutic relationships and these can be triggered in a variety of ways: a single incident within or outwith a supervision session; a misunderstanding that emerges slowly over time based on a difference of values; boundary or dual role considerations that impact detrimentally on the alliance.

> Marit has been with her supervisor Ewan for a number of years and finds it a secure and productive pairing. She also has an effective and pleasant working alliance with Kumar. They team easily and also enjoy some banter. Over a quick coffee, Kumar mentioned attending a social event with his partner, and Marit had a blinding realization that her colleague's partner was her supervisor. She said nothing, but was aware of a sinking feeling. That evening she mused over this information, feeling extremely unsettled. Her anxieties included:
>
> • feeling shocked
>
> • a sense of being betrayed
>
> ▬▶

- panicky thoughts about Kumar and Ewan sharing intimate moments and gossiping

- certainty that Kumar and Ewan must have recognized that they both knew her, given Kumar's workplace

- sensations of exclusion and feeling threatened and of boundaries being blurred

- frightening recollections of some of the opinions about the organization that she had shared with Ewan

- embarrassing memories of discussing sexuality and uncovering her attitudes towards homosexuality

- disorientation at the realization that Ewan had withheld his knowledge of her organization.

As her emotions started to subside she decided to pull her BACP 'Ethical Framework' off the shelf to see if this could sharpen up her thinking and generate a more balanced response.

Table 9.3 Application of the ethical principles

Being trustworthy: Although there is no evidence that confidentiality has been compromised, Marit is left with a strong sense that this may be the case. Ewan could not completely eradicate from his memory the material she had revealed about the organization so how could she be sure that this didn't leak out in conversations with his partner?

She remembers that they had discussed potential boundary issues/shared relationships when contracting and that none had emerged. Her trust was significantly eroded.

Were her organization aware they were paying for the professional services of an employee's partner? Was there a conflict of interest at a company level?

Marit was disappointed Ewan hadn't revealed his sexual orientation during their conversations about homosexuality and had been unable to be open with her. She realized their relationship had been less congruent and honest than she had perceived.

She felt extremely sad at the thought of losing the highly constructive elements of this supervision arrangement, which had been a transformative experience. She felt maybe there was an opportunity to rebuild trust and retain some of the benefits if Ewan could hear her concerns and if she sought supervision for organizational dilemmas elsewhere. She did feel, however, that her dealings with Kumar would need to become solely work-focused.

Autonomy: Marit felt that her autonomy had been neglected. Kumar and Ewan had chosen to not share their relationship status with her so she had been denied the opportunity to make an informed decision.

She also acknowledged that she needed to respect Kumar and Ewan's autonomy as regards choosing when and to whom they disclosed their partnership and sexual orientation.

Beneficence: Marit seriously questioned whether continuing to work with Ewan was in her best interest and thus in her clients' interest.

She also accepted that until now this supervisory pairing had served her clients well. ⮕

Table 9.3   (*continued*)

Non-maleficence: Marit felt hurt and realized her supervisory relationship had been damaged and may never recover.

She also recognized that if this difficulty could be worked through, there was a potential for learning and a deepening of the supervisory alliance, which ultimately could benefit her practice.

Justice: She felt she hadn't been treated fairly. Her view on this had not been sought and a decision made on her behalf, the weight of power residing with Ewan. He had known that a dual role existed and she hadn't. Ewan's impartiality was seriously in question.

She guessed Ewan hadn't told any of his other supervisees about his personal life, and in that sense his practice was unbiased.

Self-respect: She appreciated she had been shaken to her core and would require extra support in working through this. She was unable to turn to her usual source of back-up, her supervisor.

She began to wonder at the strength of her response and whether she was overly dependent or attached to Ewan. Perhaps she needed to address this reliance on him.

> The idea of raising the above points with Ewan filled Marit with dread. However, she felt by holding onto the memory of his trustworthiness she might find the courage to address these with him. After all, he had always encouraged her to raise any concerns.

This kind of scenario represents an acid test for any supervisory association. How this feedback is received will provide an accurate measure of the robustness of the pairing. It constitutes an opportunity for both parties to learn and for their relationship to grow. If one or other party is unable to appreciate the other's perspective and seek a way forward, the therapist can feel isolated and without the necessary resource of reliable supervision.

For Reflection

Consider the scenario outlined above:

- Are there other ethical points you can identify?
- Which aspects would you prioritize in preparing for a discussion with your supervisor?

THE IMPORTANCE OF PRACTITIONER SELF-CARE

The following section explores the specifics of how supervision can be utilized to develop practitioner self-care, in line with the ethical responsibilities discussed earlier in relation to this aspect of professional conduct.

Counsellors are often care-givers by nature with a tendency to prioritize the needs of others before their own. As such, the principle of self-care (sometimes labelled 'self-respect') highlights the need to ensure that a practitioner's own well-being is also being addressed (BACP, 2010, p. 4). By attending to this principle, the counsellor's energies can be restored so that they are able to practise at their optimum *and* enjoy their own life in a healthy and meaningful way. Supervision may focus on practitioner self-care in some of the following ways:

- monitoring personal safety
- assessing limits of professional competence
- managing a heavy client load
- scrutinizing the personal impact of complex client work
- exploring the impact of difficult personal circumstances on the counsellor and his/her practice
- taking care of counsellor and clients during organizational change or job insecurity
- identifying the re-emergence of past issues triggered by the client work
- keeping an eye on the work/life balance
- recognizing and preventing burn-out or compassion fatigue
- exploring the need to temporarily or even permanently cease practice.

A counsellor who is persistently facing difficulties either in their personal life or at their workplace may spend considerable time in supervision focusing on these issues. Although this may be indirectly beneficial to counselling practice, it can lead to more specific processing of the client work being side-lined, so during such times additional supervision may be considered. Supervision can contribute significantly to the practitioner's self-care. However, it is also essential that individuals take personal responsibility for their own well-being in all aspects of their lives.

Holistic self-care

> Shauna is a single parent who has been told that there are going to be redundancies at her practice organization. She is fearful that she may lose her job and will not be able to support her children.
>
> Lucy works at a centre for asylum seekers and works with the trauma resulting from torture and violence on a daily basis. She is becoming disassociated from her personal relationships and feels disillusioned about life. Her husband has told her that he is unhappy with their marriage and is thinking of leaving her.
>
> Jayden has just been told that his youngest son has leukaemia and will soon begin long-term cancer treatment, which is likely to be on-going for at least a year.

The counsellor may be an expert at bracketing off their own experience in the work setting, yet still faces the challenge of being emotionally and psychologically available for the client. The examples above illustrate in varying degrees some of the types of challenge that affect a practitioner's ability to be fully present with clients or to manage situations in which the client's material begins to affect them on a personal level. Supervision in these circumstances can play an invaluable role. Still, there may be long-term effects on the counsellor. The dangers of burn-out and compassion fatigue in those who work closely with vulnerable people are well documented. If symptoms are ignored, the counsellor may become increasingly diminished on a deeper level (Rothschild, 2006).

> Imagine a counsellor is like a sponge taking in water, micro-organisms and particles of dirt and dust from its surroundings. There is only so much that the sponge can hold before it becomes saturated and leaks. If left saturated for too long, it may begin to rot. The initial damage is only visible on the outside of the sponge but after some time, the sponge begins to disintegrate from the inside.

Alongside the above metaphor sits the theory of interacting parts of the self, any of which may resonate with enduring stress. The physical body may be the first to show the signs, through symptoms such as sleep disturbance, headaches or nausea. The counsellor's emotions may be characterized by a preoccupation with personal issues or client work, irritability or low mood. Alternatively, or in concert with these, there may be a growing sense of meaninglessness or futility.

Figure 9.1 depicts the relationship between the different aspects of the self that can become affected through times of personal or professional distress. If we consider that these parts of the person are intrinsically interwoven, then it figures that when one aspect is out of kilter, the others are also likely to be impacted upon at some level. In a healthy person, these aspects will be in balance with one another and the individual will be well attuned to their functioning – knowing when and how to respond if an imbalance is experienced.

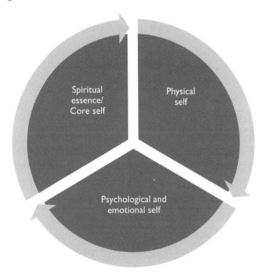

Figure 9.1 Aspects of the self

> Rachael has been managing a difficult personal situation for several months and has worked with Carl, her supervisor, to monitor the impact of this on her practice and to ensure that she has adequate self-care strategies in place. Each month she assures Carl that she is coping with the situation and that she is still working effectively. One day, Carl receives a telephone call from Rachael's partner cancelling her next supervision session. Rachael has been taken ill and the doctors think she could be suffering from M.E.

We all have the ability to delude ourselves and others into thinking that we are OK even when deep down we are not. This is especially true when work or personal pressures come on slowly and then persist in the background like a dripping tap. The counsellor's sense of responsibility, both at home and in practice, drives them on to keep going. It may be possible to continue to operate reasonably well under stress, but in an attempt to keep one's head above water, functioning may become somewhat superficial. The danger here is that we may over time, and without realizing, cease to be fully in touch with ourselves. In turn, our ability to be truly present with clients, to connect with the here-and-now experience in therapy, to empathize and to make informed decisions may all be diminished. Likewise, we may not be able to fully engage with our supervisor and so the knock-on effect continues.

The BACP Ethical Framework states that counsellors should aspire to:

- 'resilience – the capacity to work with clients' concerns without being personally diminished
- humility – the ability to assess accurately and acknowledge one's own strengths and weaknesses
- wisdom – possession of sound judgement that informs practice' (BACP, 2010, p. 4).

The exercise of these qualities may under normal circumstances pose no concern. At more demanding times, the supervisor becomes a key agent enabling a counsellor to recognize the signs that certain personal resources are in significantly short supply. It is important to take heed of the observations s/he offers. The situation may be more complex and the risks greater if the organization is under strain or the supervisor herself is suffering from stress. Then, the chance that signs of depletion in the counsellor will be recognized is likely to be reduced.

> In supervision Shirley was exploring a general sense of weariness. Work had been exceptionally busy and there were difficulties at home too. As she talked, she realized she hadn't been to her yoga class for several weeks now and couldn't remember when she had last spent time pottering in her garden, one of her favourite activities. Even her dogs were getting short shrift with the briefest of walks each day.

For Reflection

Take a look at the following areas of your life and ask yourself if you are engaging in these as much as normal:

- Quality time with friends and family
- Looking after your physical well-being
- Looking after your spiritual well-being.

Liz was working with a number of depressed clients and her supervisor noticed a growing apathy in her over the months. Liz denied any such impact and insisted that she was fine. It was only when she started to feel really down herself that she recognized there might be a connection. She became more aware of the physical and emotional responses that she was experiencing both during and after counselling sessions. From this point on she rigorously adopted strategies to ground herself and shake off her clients' energies. She also learnt the warning signs, such as a reduction in her normal level of physical activity, and that she needed to listen to observations from her supervisor. Liz was reminded that taking part in regular outdoor activities helps her to maintain a connection with her sense of self.

The idea that emotions and experiences can be held within the body has been widely acknowledged – although some counsellors may struggle to accept the validity of this concept until life events inform them of its truth (Gendlin, 1979; King, 2004; Totton, 2005). Some argue that physical sensations experienced during the therapeutic work may be an indicator that transpersonal energies are being absorbed from clients and so cleansing the therapeutic space and engaging in personal 'psychic protection' may form an important part of the self-care regime (Clarkson, 2002, p. 128). Whether you perceive such somatic responses as some form of transpersonal phenomenon or if you settle for an entirely different explanation is not important. What does matter is listening to the body's communication of 'dis-ease'. In Western culture, the body is often considered to have a separate identity, living an almost shadow-like existence and holding onto emotions that are all too often being ignored (Eiden, 1998). The supervisor may be able to help the counsellor to bring into awareness their somatic responses to the work and to develop and monitor self-care strategies. As most practitioners only meet with their supervisor once a month, this process may only attend to the immediate, more practical side of self-care and so adopting methods to connect with the body and monitor one's own self-care at depth on a regular basis is essential.

For Reflection

- What sensations do I feel in my body with my clients/this client/in this work situation?
- What might my body be telling me? What might these sensations mean?
- Is there anything I need to do now to take greater care of myself?
- I can't feel anything – why might this be? Is there anything that I need to do to reconnect with my body?

Finally, it feels important to consider the meaning we ascribe to therapeutic work. Although counselling is a rewarding profession, the motivation for our involvement is only in part altruistic. Most practitioners admit to benefitting from their clients on a personal as well as a professional level. There are dangers, however, if the key driver lies in our need to nurture ourselves in some way, to boost our own self-esteem or to distract attention from our own concerns. Seeking out the most complex and hard-to-help clients with little consideration of the personal impact may be an indicator of what could be termed 'martyr syndrome'. This can be endemic within some organizations, with what amounts to unspoken competition to be the one with the largest or most demanding caseload or else to be the most empathic towards distressed individuals. If we are only attending to the part of ourselves that seeks to feel better through our good actions towards others, then we are probably ignoring other aspects of self-care, with consequent risks to our integrity and connection to ourselves.

For Reflection

Has my supervisor noticed anything different about me, my way of being and/or what I am doing?

What strategies do I have in place to look after:

- My psychological and emotional self?
- My physical self?
- My sense of myself?

Are any aspects being ignored?

What might help me to maintain a regular routine with these strategies?

IN SUMMARY

The need to make ethically informed decisions runs through much of the activity in supervision. Explicit definition of the ethical principles involved in a demanding therapy situation can identify the source of practitioner tension, bring conceptual clarity, and point the way to appropriate action. The factors in play may well include those associated with organizational pressure or the influence of a political agenda. Issues for consideration extend to the framework and interior of the supervisory relationship itself, requiring the same capacity for ethical mindfulness as do interactions with clients.

Attention to counsellor self-care needs to be in evidence in the discussion of possible responses: as with the other principles, there are times when its claims have to be prioritized. Maintenance of the counsellor's mental and emotional health is an undeniable prerequisite for the exercise of effective professional activity. In this area the potential contribution of supervision is clear.

Recommended reading

Bloom, W. (2006) *Psychic Protection: Creating Positive Energies for People and Places* (London: Piatkus).

Gendlin, E. (1979) *Focusing* (New York: Everest House).

Mearns, D. (2008) 'How Much Supervision Should You Have?' *BACP Information Sheet (S1)* (Lutterworth: BACP).

Rothschild, B. (2006) *Help for the Helper: The Psychophysiology of Compassion Fatigue and Vicarious Trauma* (London: W.W. Norton & Co.).

Chapter 10

Present and Future

INTRODUCTION

In 1964 the BBC broadcast the first in what has become a regular series of programmes based on the lives of a group of people, just seven years old at the time, and who were subsequently interviewed at intervals of seven years. The trajectories of these lives – a mix of satisfactions, sadness and the just plain ordinary stories of what it is to be human – could scarcely have been predicted half a century ago, any more than we can be clear what the future holds for the counselling profession and for us as individuals.

Acknowledging the fallibilities of prediction, this chapter defines the stage on which the coming years of the profession are likely to play out. It looks at the social and philosophical climate; at influences on careers in counselling; at contemporary meanings ascribed to ill-health and wellness; at technological innovation; and at the role which research is likely to play in shaping the profession.

The social, political and economic framework is inescapably influential. Economic recession and government cutbacks have impacted on the lives of whole sectors of the population not just through the experience of financial hardship, but through the emotional consequences of low income, unemployment and inadequate housing. What counsellors take to supervision may well include frustration at what they see as the loss of adequate services and subsequent denial of opportunity for their clients. Unlike most managers or political and business leaders, counsellors meet and resonate with distressed individuals every day of their working lives. The ability to empathize may well add to the counsellor's sense of impotence and irritation – natural and (arguably) necessary responses, which supervision may provide the space to verbalize and address.

Political rhetoric is often difficult to translate into meaningful understandings when it comes to interactions with clients. Encouragement to greater

self-responsibility – one of the guiding principles of the current UK government – accords well with the counsellor's ambition to facilitate self-directed,
autonomous responses. Conflict or feelings of guilt or inadequacy may arise
for the counsellor, however, when it is evident that in practical terms the odds
are increasingly stacked against the client being able to direct his own life.

> Barbara has been seeing Chris in the city-centre counselling agency
> where she has a placement. At times Chris, who worked in a factory
> for 30 years until it closed two years ago, has flashes of optimism
> about finding another job. Both of them know that the employment
> market is especially unfavourable for older males. He has kept a log
> of his unsuccessful applications – over 100 so far. His relationship
> with his wife has deteriorated in the meantime: he regards her as
> unsupportive of his efforts. Both of them are highly anxious that the
> mortgage company will re-possess their home, on which they have
> a large outstanding loan. Barbara needed regular supervision on her
> work with Chris, partly to address her own sense of inadequacy. She
> felt that she should be doing more to help Chris, and that his inability
> to obtain work implied a failure on her part.

Counsellors can also feel the sting of the prevailing climate of bureaucrati-
zation, in which good intentions to address social ills have sometimes become
legalistic rods with which to beat almost anyone within reach. The school
setting can be especially trying to those supporting young people: excessive
anxiety about health and safety legislation and the need to attend to child protection policies can inhibit the development of challenging educational programmes and cast a shadow over therapeutic relationships. The counsellor,
aware of the need to work within institutional and legal frameworks, can
sometimes feel opposing loyalties – to the client, to significant others in the
client's life, to the organization and to other professionals. Attending to the
well-being of one person or group can feel like neglecting the interests of others.

> Martin appreciated that Nicole's long history of depression had
> been a major factor in Social Services' decision to remove her four
> children from her care. Yet as her counsellor he was confronted
> at every meeting with her profound sense of loss as well as her
> apparent impotence in the face of the legal mechanisms in which
> she was now inescapably embroiled. In supervision he found
> himself giving voice to the anger he felt at the breaking up of
> Nicole's family and its effect on all the family members. He was
> angry too at what he perceived as capricious, legalistic behaviour
> on the part of the social workers involved.

Since the position from which we work brings an expectation of openness and engagement with clients, the corollary of strong feelings on the part of the counsellor is, at times, inevitable. When my chronically ill client's Disability Living Allowance is stopped; when he is receiving threatening letters from the Department for Work and Pensions; when he fears even more scrutiny and investigations; when his health is deteriorating through the stress of it all – I am unlikely to remain untouched. Supervision may not be – and isn't – a panacea. But it is a place to go.

THE CONTEXT

It is a truism that supervisor and supervisee swim in the same waters. Or rather, it is preferable that they should do so at least some of the time. The temperature, the clarity or murkiness, the rough or smooth surface, the currents and under-currents: all will be felt by the supervisee. Better that the supervisor has experience of what it feels like. Extending the metaphor a little further, the counsellor needs a supervisor who hears and responds when s/he is in fear of drowning – though not to be accompanied in succumbing to the waves.

Life's synchronicities could bring together a supervisee whose agency is closing with a supervisor whose service is struggling with financial cutbacks. The counsellor's client base, like that of the trainee Barbara above, could well include individuals facing the impacts of redundancy. At such times, the sensitivities of the parties to supervision need to be especially well honed. Every pairing will manage this differently, but better to share honestly as much information as is relevant and to agree to keep each other apprised of developments which might change the nature (or the survival) of the supervision relationship.

The utility of supervisee and supervisor having shared awareness of the external context can be illustrated by imagining its absence. For either party to lack a level of basic understanding of the current delivery mechanisms of mental health services such as IAPT, of professional registration and accreditation, of ethical and legal frameworks, would suggest a lack of attention to significant aspects of context. As part of the educative agenda of supervision, it is entirely appropriate for the supervisee to raise these and similar areas for discussion. It may well be that what follows includes research in journals or on the internet, or a phone call to the information line of the professional association.

Equally as significant as the practicalities of organizational or institutional developments are the social and philosophical trends which underpin them. Every age of humankind has its prevailing doctrine: ours rides – on the surface at least – on a well-established belief in the pre-eminence of empirical science over the 'felt senses'. Hence, statutory mental health funding in the UK follows the same lines of approval (via the NICE guidelines) as resourcing for physical healthcare. The mechanisms of psychological assessment, diagnosis and treatment within the NHS are heavily influenced by the medical model, never mind that empiricism and mental health are an ill-assorted couple. Quantification frequently dominates formal systems of evaluation, with qualitative measures judged a poor relation. There will be major challenges for the parties to supervision to explore tenable responses where the demands of the working context do not match the beliefs of the practitioner – or else fail to meet the expressed needs of clients. For example, a respectful assessment strategy can be developed which is more involving of the client – a strategy which promotes the therapeutic alliance at the same time as finding formulations which are less stigmatizing. Where a supervisee is providing a manualized intervention, supervision can support the practitioner in devising ways to individualize the approach. BACP's Counselling for Depression programme is an example of a manualized approach which seeks to do just this (BACP, 2012c).

The social climate in which counselling and psychotherapy have developed has given these activities a mixed reception, with scepticism and stigma never far away. Whilst North American culture embraced the talking therapies more readily, in the UK their acceptance as legitimate strands of intervention has progressed slowly. Campaigns by Mind, Time to Change and other mental health charities continue to challenge social prejudice and to encourage open debate about the need for better understanding and provision. The current government has declared in its document *No Health without Mental Health* (HMSO, 2010) the importance of attention to emotional and psychological well-being – both of the individual and of society at large. 'Following the recession, it is clear that we need to heal emotional wounds, which means that we are looking for a psychological recovery alongside our economic recovery', writes the Minister of State for Care Services in the preface to *Talking Therapies: A Four Year Plan of Action* (Department of Health, 2011, p. 2). The Health & Social Care Act 2012 incorporates specific mention of the equal status of physical and mental healthcare.

Workers in the sector know that the political rhetoric isn't yet matched on the ground. *Talking Therapies* (cited above) promises a level of investment such that by 2014/15 'every adult that requires it should have access to psychological therapies to treat anxiety disorders or depression'. Central government ambition is clear: 'We can no longer have a health service that treats people physically but leaves them struggling mentally' (ibid.). A report by the London School of Economics (LSE, 2012, p. 1) shows how far the reality is from the aspiration: 'It is a real scandal that we have 6 million people with depression or crippling anxiety conditions and 700,000 children with problem behaviours, anxiety or depression', state its authors. 'Yet three-quarters of each group get no treatment.'

The precise role of supervision in all of this still remains to be defined. There is no suggestion from any of the major professional associations that supervision will be quietly side-lined. If anything, the concern to foreground ethical practice makes the activity ever more relevant. BACP is currently engaged in a project to review the Roth & Pilling (2008) Supervision Competences and develop a supervision training curriculum. The likelihood is that moves to accredit supervisors and supervision training programmes will gain ground.

The proliferation of activities in which the use of counselling skills is a requirement adds a further dimension to an already complex landscape. A typical example of such a role is provided by the staff support worker for one of the major train companies who offers incident debriefing to employees. She is daily in contact with colleagues needing to talk about a whole range of experiences – anything from dealing with a violent or abusive passenger to a death on the line. Her need for appropriate access to supervision is no less than that of a counsellor – even though her role title is different and her work is embedded in the day-to-day working of the organization (McLeod, 2008).

Though bold claims may be made for the impact of supervision (including those made in this book), the supervisory dyad is not in itself in a position to change political and legislative frameworks. By contrast, the professional associations have more leverage and more access to policy makers. BACP have collaborated productively with the Council for Healthcare Regulatory Excellence (now re-named the Professional Standards Authority for Health and Social Care) to establish a mechanism for voluntary registration which meets the requirements of the 2012 Act. Dialogue with government is increasingly more meaningful and productive.

The supervision room may seem a world away from the rough and tumble of parliamentary process or the deliberations of governmental institutions. Better, though, that counsellor and supervisor take good account of emerging events in the wider arena, so as to be responsive to their impact. If registration and chartered status are to be the touchstones for formally sanctioned practice, then discussions of routes to access, applications, and the strengthening of the professional profile belong in the supervision space.

In the highly competitive world of mental health provision, it is critical that the counsellor be as well placed as possible to secure a properly funded and tenured position.

At its heart, both counselling and supervision provide an experience paradoxically rare in contemporary life. The world is full of talk – through the audio-visual media, via an unparalleled array of printed text, words that come at us via e-mail, social networking sites and the mushroom growth of the internet. Missing, though, is access to what Banning (2012, p. 19) calls 'transformative conversations': proper dialogue which helps us understand who we are, what we value and how to set about fashioning a meaningful life. In seeking to support good practice in supervision, we are also promoting a better quality of dialogue between human beings.

FINANCE AND CAREERS

As with any professional training, the business of becoming a counsellor has considerable costs in terms of time, energy and money. Living expenses have to be met over a four or five year training period in which there is normally no income prior to qualification. In addition to funding the course fees, trainees pay for regular supervision – and often for personal counselling – throughout the duration of the course. It is an expensive few years and excludes those who cannot afford it or who are unable to access funding. Even after becoming qualified, supervision must be paid for even if working as a volunteer or unpaid associate. Unlike with many other professions, counselling has no established career route and no national pay scale, so that questions inevitably arise about the degree to which counsellors can be expected to contribute without security of income or agreed professional status.

The multiplicity of qualifications and standards in training in counselling and psychotherapy has been one of the barriers in the way of establishing a national career framework. Recent initiatives have begun to tackle the problems of such a varied provision, and should eventually lead to formally agreed structures and professional pathways. The Quality Assurance Agency for Higher Education, whose role is to define and uphold quality and standards in UK universities and colleges, has recently published benchmarks for counselling and psychotherapy as a point of reference for entry level to the profession, for the benefit of the aspiring therapist, future employers and the public. Voluntary registration, mentioned above, represents another step towards formalizing entry levels for counselling and psychotherapy and – eventually – standardizing pay levels.

The different sectors in which counsellors work present their own demands on the practitioner, some involving additional training and all requiring the development of specialist expertise. There is an increasing call for counselling for young people. The initiative of the Welsh Assembly provides a model for the principle of a counsellor in every school. Prisons counselling – still a Cinderella service – is beginning to articulate the particular ethical and professional challenges experienced by its members: a huge unmet need faces any government willing to acknowledge the enormity of the task.

The move in the NHS to introduce AQP (Any Qualified Provider) status will require agencies in that marketplace to provide evidence of organizational competencies and qualifications of every counsellor employed or contracted. Larger providers, such as EAPs and NHS psychology services, are already positioned to fulfil the requirements to be a qualified provider. Smaller independent agencies and self-employed and freelance practitioners are being encouraged to form local groups, which could offer a wide range of training and expertise, and thereby promote the principle of client choice.

This book has encouraged supervisees to use supervision to talk through issues and problems, to gain new perspectives, and to develop creative ways of working to reduce constraints or to work within them more effectively. The developing social and political climate makes all of this even more relevant if the profession is committed to maintaining and improving counselling services and honouring the right to high quality therapy from ethical and competent counsellors and supervisors. With this background in mind, discussions in supervision could well address questions such as:

■ What issues and problems do you face in your professional work with respect to adequacy of resources and the consequences?
■ To what extent are you aware of the specific repercussions of these on clients and services?
■ How might you contribute to developing your service or entering new areas of practice?
■ Where do you obtain support and information?
■ Which battles have you won and which lost?
■ What is your field of influence and how might you extend this?

The last of these questions might be met with a blank response. When faced with apparently 'done deals' it may be hard to manage the sense of powerlessness: decision-making may appear to take little account of client (or counsellor) welfare. Whatever the context, the commitment of counsellors and supervisors remains to:

- develop our understanding of the complexity of organizational issues and seek to understand the demands on the organization
- be aware of the need for developing systems of evaluation and cost-effective practices
- identify the possible consequences of planned actions
- resource our arguments with support from the professional body and, where available, from published work and research
- offer suggestions about possible alternatives where decisions seem to us in conflict with clients' interests
- notify the professional body of significant events
- access legal and professional advice services where necessary
- use supervision, colleagues and helplines to work through difficulties and options for action.

ORGANIZATIONAL RESPONSES

Earlier chapters have presented examples of ethical and practical dilemmas facing the supervisee in an organizational context. Tensions are unlikely to disappear between the supervisee's concern to promote client welfare and organizational preoccupation with outcomes and efficiency. In many services, high numbers of referrals lead to lengthy waiting lists, which sit uneasily with the requirement to allocate an appointment within a short time frame. Feeling a responsibility for the client once in the system can create pressure to make an initial assessment even though the therapy cannot begin for weeks or months. For the counsellor, this can generate a conveyor belt-like sensation, with little space for reflection and recuperation.

Funding regimes can exacerbate these same issues. Local or macro-political decisions about which client group is funded and the level of financing affects provision and counsellor salaries – as well as the contribution made towards supervision costs. Fund-holders typically define service norms and criteria, sometimes making an uneasy fit with the beliefs and values of staff.

Independent counsellors, meanwhile, face a different set of challenges. They may have more freedom to determine their contacts with clients, length of the contract and focus of the work – but another set of responsibilities enters the frame. Administrative and practical problems and the whole range of lone-worker issues – anything from room booking to legal status to the fundamental need to have sufficient income – become the concern of the individual. There may be no peers with whom to discuss day-to-day concerns. Supervision can be a key element in ensuring against professional isolation.

Supervisee-centred versus organization-centred approaches

Supervisee-centred approaches to supervision acknowledge that expertise is located in the counsellor, so that the supervisor's task is to facilitate what is to be revealed. Merry (1999, p. 141) talks of the application of 'expertise, knowledge and experience as a "co-worker" in the pursuit of deeper understanding'. The actualizing tendency of the individual practitioner, and the principles enshrined in the therapeutic conditions, are paramount as are exploration of ethical and practice issues and clarification of understanding. In such collaborative enquiry 'both people in supervision are self-directed and can contribute equally to the process'. Cognitive and intuitive knowing are equally valued.

The supervisor working within an organization-centred model takes responsibility for ensuring that the session meets the requirements of the service. There is a general expectation of observance of organizational norms and adherence to a set of published standards and outcomes. Some practitioners prefer to work within set structures which, for them, provide the security of knowing that all eventualities are covered and accountability is ensured. The down side of such practice is that the applied structure can take precedence, and that an external locus of evaluation replaces the judgement and experience of the professional.

The culture of management by measure risks denying the uniqueness of each client, each counsellor and the relationship between them. De Board (1990, p. 123) discusses ways in which individuals and groups use 'being organised' as a defence against anxiety and cites Menzies' (1979) claim that 'ritual task performance' constitutes a method of protection from the anxiety of patient care and decision-making in hospitals. The behaviours she observed ensured individuals were 'taught to follow an extremely rigid task list' which, whilst apparently assisting people and the organization to feel safer, 'actively discouraged (student) nurses from using their discretion and initiative'. Craib (1994, p. 40) describes this need for uniformity and safety as resulting in 'cutting out gingerbread men': in denying our anxiety about getting it right or our disappointment about not having got it right, we create everyone in the same mould or force them to conform to someone else's norms.

Building on potential

Counsellor supervision is a complex combination of relationships, tasks and processes. This book has promoted the view of supervision as a vehicle for working out what is most useful to clients and for managing the counsellor's accountability to clients, organizations, themselves and the profession in efficient, ethical and creative ways. We have championed the capacity of the individual to take personal responsibility for their role as a practitioner, and have encouraged supervisees to challenge and be open to challenge.

The reality may be very different. Pressures to conform may result in a more directive – even dictatorial – way of providing supervision in which the supervisee can feel criticized and judged inadequate if presenting anything less than 'idealized' practice. A place of safety in which to discuss doubts, concerns and questions may be replaced by a climate of anxiety, withholding and self-protective behaviours.

The sum experience of supervision needs to strengthen counsellors' belief in their competence. This does not imply that any of us is ever a 'fully-formed practitioner' – since, like the concept of self-actualization, this elusive status is an idea to be worked with as competences continually extend and develop. There is little doubt that supervisees can support the growth of a climate of potential in the supervision room by developing a balanced view of their own skills and capacities. Reading, attendance at seminars, discussions with reliable peers, taking account of feedback from clients: all can contribute to promoting a grounded concept of the self as practitioner. Both supervisee and supervisor share in the business of deepening experience and understanding; both can contribute to the honest and sensitive exploration of today's practice so as to add to the quality of tomorrow's work.

MENTAL HEALTH AND MENTAL ILLNESS: A CHOICE OF POSITION

Discussion above has proposed the use of supervision to devise alternative ways in which aspects of a service (such as assessment and evaluation) may be approached. The setting in which the supervisee practises – organizational, social, financial – will be heavily influential on his day-to-day activity. So too – though at a subtler level – is the conceptual basis which underpins the therapeutic work. It is reasonable to expect that this conceptual foundation will feature in the supervision dialogue, since the whole enterprise of therapy is predicated on what the counsellor believes his work is about.

Put simply, the two most starkly contrasting contemporary positions are, on the one hand, the symptom-based approach to mental ill-health and, on the other, a holistic understanding of mental and emotional wellness. Both positions have been ably described in the last decade, the proponents of each developing more precise definitions of their theoretical framework.

The clearest example of the former position is provided by the most recent draft of the *Diagnostic and Statistical Manual of Mental Disorders* (American Psychiatric Association, 2013). This document, updated at intervals since 1952 by the American Psychiatric Association, and now into its fifth revision, extends the process of fragmentation and medicalization of human behaviour considerably further than in its previous iterations. To its critics, amongst whom number the British Psychological Society, only biological and neurological factors have been considered by the authors as valid contributors to the swathe of problem behaviours now identified as pathological. Social and environmental causation appears to be absent from the conceptualization. Furthermore, a whole range of responses are now labelled in the draft text as 'abnormal' which many people would assert to be simply part of being human, such as a pattern of argumentative, defiant or headstrong behaviour in young people, or mood swings, irritability or tension in premenstrual women (Jackson, 2012).

A radical alternative to the DSM approach can be found in the wellness movement established in the English-speaking countries since the 1980s, and predicated on an impressive body of (mostly North American) research undertaken over the last half-century. The beginning of the new millennium was marked by World Mental Health Day 2000 drawing on the statement from the UK Health Education Authority that mental health 'is more than an absence of symptoms of mental health and distress'. The statement's authors assert that mental health resides in 'the emotional and spiritual resilience which enables us to enjoy life and survive pain, disappointment and sadness. It is a positive sense of well-being and an underlying belief in our own, and others', dignity and worth' (HEA, 2000, p. 1). Ten years later, the UK government announced its intention to ask the Office of National Statistics to produce measures to implement the Prime Minister's ambition of gauging 'general well-being'. In the previous year, two Nobel economists had called on world leaders to move away from using orthodox measures such as gross domestic product and to move instead to evaluating well-being and sustainability (*The Guardian*, 2010). The Health and Wellbeing Boards being set up as part of the changes to NHS governance provide, in principle at least, further impetus to this movement.

Supervision is unlikely to devote time to investigating political niceties. It is, however, an arena in which supervisees can air their thoughts and their questions about the direction and aims – about 'the point' – of the therapy.

Do counsellor and client share the view, stated or assumed, that the therapy exists primarily to extinguish or reduce unwanted thoughts and behaviours, or that its intention is a generalized move towards a heightened state of wellness, or a combination of these? The choice of philosophical position is for the individual practitioner, who may be negotiating the stretch between working in a symptom-reduction programme and a personal belief in a holistic concept of wellness.

TECHNOLOGICAL INNOVATION

The range of applications (apps) accessible via phones, laptops and tablets/pads offers a new generation of resources for therapeutic support. Some counselling services, notably in educational settings, already provide digital self-help information. For this and future generations, apps have the possibility of replacing self-help leaflets, books and tapes. This facility has the potential not only to relieve over-subscribed services but may alter or replace the current provision. The extent to which they become an alternative to or an adjunct of counselling may depend on how counsellors embrace this technology as another aspect of working with clients. For people who feel embarrassed about seeking face to face help these apps already provide an opportunity to see problems as not uncommon and to obtain help otherwise difficult to access.

Available in Android and iphone, itouch and ipad formats, apps include a wide variety of self-help advice on subjects such as health and fitness, relaxation techniques, managing stress and anxiety. Many counsellors already recommend paper versions of similar material when it is likely that a client could find them of use. There are apps for more specific areas of therapeutic work such as CBT-based interventions for mental health problems, stress management and 'reframing' and for post-trauma symptoms. Research is being done on providing structured self-help processes in apps for 'social anxiety' to aid university students (Topham, 2012).

Among the questions raised by the technology are those concerning the primacy of the therapeutic relationship. If the evidence from counselling research is that the relationship is a key feature in the healing process, what are the implications for programmes which do not involve any kind of meeting of two persons? Research is just beginning into the impact of models of helping which, rather than harnessing the relationship between therapist and client, rely on following instructions and on taking responsibility for managing one's own therapeutic journey.

Supervision could support the counsellor with:

- discussing and understanding the juxtaposition of apps and counselling – if, when and how they could be an asset or a hindrance to the counselling process
- the development or protection of client autonomy
- decision-making about if and when to introduce specific apps
- helping clients to make choices on the appropriateness of which application could be of best use for their life at this point and/or in specific parts of the process of counselling
- exploring the effects on the relationship between client and counsellor
- further development of apps appropriate to counselling or supervision.

RESEARCH

The significance of research in the world of the counsellor is increasing rapidly. Member associations consistently promote the role of research-based activity as a key element in the development of the profile of the profession. The individual supervisee's experience of this activity will depend on training, context and personal preference. Many courses promote the role of research in the curriculum and require students to become familiar with its methods and products. For some practitioners, research and evaluation constitute a staple component of the working environment.

Studies into the process and outcomes of supervision itself have provided a base of evidence to support arguments for its effectiveness. In their systematic review, Wheeler & Richards (2007, p. 63) identified a range of findings demonstrating the benefit to the supervisee, such as the importance of the supervisory relationship, the development of self-awareness, competency and the 'self-efficacy' of the counsellor. However, evidence for the extent of positive outcomes for clients remains limited: their review, they state, 'identified substantial gaps in the evidence-base on supervision' and there were 'many methodological problems'. Many studies remain to be done, particularly in this area of tracking the influence of supervision on the counselling process.

Whilst it is important to distinguish practitioner from academic supervision (required by the researcher), the counsellor's engagement in research and evaluation may still enter the regular supervision space. Counsellors may well want to discuss some of the doubts, questions and dilemmas which involvement in research and evaluation brings. Where the supervisor is herself research active, the supervisee may be able to tap in to some of that experience, the educative component of supervision being extended to encompass situations where therapeutic work and formal study of the work overlap.

Supervisees may be required to or may choose to be involved in research. There are strong arguments for each of a range of paradigms – from orthodox methods, such as randomized control trials, through to individual data gathering. Some of the newer research paradigms may appeal more to the practitioner whose talents lie principally in the day-to-day delivery of therapy. Working in a peer group (such as a peer supervision group) or undertaking more formalized team-based practitioner research studies can utilize the variety of experience and knowledge, contribute to the development of its members and add credibility to process and findings as compared to a single practitioner case study (McLeod, 2010). Practice research networks bring researchers and therapists together to collaborate in naturalistic psychotherapy studies in which understandings from the day-to-day work of the counsellor can be made available to a wider audience (Henton & Midgley, 2011).

Using supervision to develop research awareness can help define issues and themes. The inclusion of the supervisor in this process provides a witness to the supervisee's experiences, as the following example illustrates:

> In talking through her work with a client in supervision Jean admitted to feeling frustrated whilst with her client and was interested to hear that her supervisor expressed a feeling of sadness as she presented her client work. After a pause, she realized she had been working hard to help her client to gain immediate help and comfort and missed the depth of distress the client was experiencing. 'I avoided facing and acknowledging the severity of his pain. I was rescuing and he must not have felt heard by me.'
>
> This insight led her to be acutely aware of changing her ways of listening more and interacting differently. Subsequently this sparked an interest in Jean to look for research on counsellor 'Achilles heel' moments, how they are discovered in supervision, and how they affect the relationship and outcomes in therapy. She used some supervision time thereafter to give attention to questions in her practice arising from this insight.
>
> After about a year, she and her supervisor collaborated on a journal article based on their combined notes and reflections.

The interface of research activity and supervision may, in some circumstances, be as significant as it became for Jean. To develop 'research mindedness' practitioners can ask themselves: What interests me about the interactions between this client and myself? What might it be useful for me to understand about her or his issues? How does what I discover in supervision affect my clients? Arranging time in supervision to explore and create meanings in the complexities of client and counsellor interactions, and to identify specific areas of interest, utilizes the supervisor's experience in an area of shared curiosity, and can help enhance awareness of the field and increase knowledge of available sources.

Reflection on what is being taken into client work will be helped by brief notes following on from supervision. Noting the impact that supervision had on the therapy session can prompt further questions to take back to supervision. Further reading around the topic, and accessing the latest research findings in professional journals and articles in newspapers by social, medical and health journalists, will enrich learning and can enhance the counsellor's understanding as well as benefitting the wider community.

AN ASPIRATION THAT ENDURES

The ambition of this book has been to stimulate creativity as well as to reinforce commitment to the educational, management and support tasks of supervision. Counsellor and supervisor hold joint responsibility for engaging in an activity which should be critical to the enduring success of the therapy. With client welfare as the centre of concern, there is the opportunity to combine wisdom, knowledge and experience – the felt sense just as much as what is cognitively evident. Respect for oneself and for one's fellow professional is matched by respect for the client and what s/he is seeking to achieve. There are few clear-cut answers, but a host of possibilities, of hunches and of clues which feed in to the therapeutic process. The process is safe because it is held by an ethical and professional framework defining the key aspects of the interaction: client autonomy; proper attention to risk; fairness; trustworthiness; appropriate counsellor self-care.

As with so much else in life, there is no end point to the journey of supervision. Time shared on the professional road between supervisee and supervisor may not always feel productive, or the direction may not be obvious. Tolerance of frustration or of a circuitous route may be a necessary ingredient. Yet the sum of the supervisee's experience, if it is to inform her or his therapeutic work, needs to be positive and energizing. The conversations are limited in time and in scope, though learning about interactions and what makes human beings what they are could continue for many lifetimes. Supervision, at its best, is a place where both parties add breadth and depth to their learning, and are reminded that they want to learn more.

Recommended reading

Bower, P. (2010) 'Evidence Based Practice in Counselling and Psychotherapy' *BACP Information Sheet (R2)* (Lutterworth: BACP).

Cooper, M. (2011) 'Meeting the Demand for Evidence-Based Practice' *Therapy Today*, 22 (4),10–16.

Glossary of Abbreviations and Organizations

AFT Association for Family Therapy, www.aft.org.uk, 7 Executive Suite, St James Court, Wilderspool Causeway, Warrington, Cheshire WA4 6PS.

BABCP British Association for Behavioural and Cognitive Psychotherapies, www.babcp.com, Imperial House, Hornby St., Bury, Lancs BL9 5BN, 0161 705 4304.

BACP British Association for Counselling & Psychotherapy, www.bacp.co.uk, BACP House, 15 St John's Business Park, Lutterworth LE17 4HB, 01455 883300.

BAP British Association of Psychotherapists, www.bap-psychotherapy.org, 37 Mapesbury Road, London NW2 4HJ, 020 8452 9823.

BAPT British Association of Play Therapists, www.bapt.info, 31 Cedar Drive, Bristol BS31 2TY, 01179 860390.

BASRT British Association for Sexual & Relationship Therapy; now COSRT (see below).

BPS British Psychological Society, www.bps.org.uk, St Andrews House, 48 Princess Road East, Leicester LE1 7DR, 0116 254 9568.

COSCA Counselling & Psychotherapy in Scotland, www.cosca.org.uk, 16 Melville Terrace, Stirling FK8 2NE, 01786 475140.

COSRT College of Sexual and Relationship Therapists, PO Box 13686, London SW20 9ZH, info@cosrt.org.uk, 020 8543 2707.

EAP Employee Assistance Programme.

FDAP Federation of Drug & Alcohol Professionals, www.fdap.org.uk, Unit 11A Cannon Wharf Business Centre, 35 Evelyn Street, London SE8 5RT, 0207 237 3399 or 01636 612590.

NICE National Institute for Health and Clinical Excellence.

P&W model The reference in the small ad is to Page, S. & Wosket, V. (2001) *Supervising the Counsellor: A Cyclical Model*, 2nd edn (London: Routledge). The text is based on the Cyclical model devised by the authors.

PTUK Play Therapy UK, ptukorg@aol.com, The Coach House, Belmont Road, Uckfield, East Sussex TH22 1BP, 01825 761143.

SIGN   Scottish Intercollegiate Guidelines Network.

UKAHPP   UK Association for Humanistic Psychology Practitioners, www.ahpp.org, Box BCM AHPP, London WC1N 3XX.

UKCP   United Kingdom Council for Psychotherapy, www.ukcp.org.uk, 2nd Floor, Edward House, 2 Wakley Street, London EC1V 7LT, 020 7014 9955.

UKRCP   United Kingdom Register of Counsellors/Psychotherapists. Registration is open to accredited members of BACP, COSCA, FDAP and UKAHPP.

Bibliography

American Psychiatric Association (2013) *Diagnostic and Statistical Manual of Mental Disorders*, 5th edn (Washington, DC: American Psychiatric Association).

BACP (2009) *Guidelines for Online Counselling and Psychotherapy*, 3rd edn (Lutterworth: BACP).

BACP (2010) *Ethical Framework for Good Practice in Counselling and Psychotherapy* (Lutterworth: BACP).

BACP (2012a) *What is Counselling? It's Good to Talk*, www.bacp.co.uk/admin/structure/files/pdf/7461_gtt_briefing.pdf, accessed 5 September 2012.

BACP (2012b) *BACP: Accreditation*, www.bacp/co.uk/accreditation, accessed 20 September 2012.

BACP (2012c) *Counselling for Depression (CfD)*, www.bacp.co.uk/learning/Counselling%20for%20Depression/, accessed 18 September 2012.

Banning, N. (2012) 'Who Wants To Be a Counsellor?' *Therapy Today*, 23 (5), 16–19.

Bion, W. (1961) *Experiences in Groups* (New York: Basic Books).

Bloom, W. (2006) *Psychic Protection: Creating Positive Energies for People and Places* (London: Piatkus).

Bolton, G. (2005) *Reflective Practice: Writing and Professional Development*, 2nd edn (London: Sage).

Bond, T. (2009) *Standards and Ethics for Counselling in Action*, 3rd edn (London: Sage).

Bond, T. & Sandu, A. (2005) *Therapists in Court* (London: Sage).

Borders, D. L. & Brown, L. L. (2005) *The New Handbook of Counseling Supervision* (New York: Lawrence Erlbaum Associates).

Bower, P. (2010) 'Evidence Based Practice in Counselling and Psychotherapy' *BACP Information Sheet (R2)* (Lutterworth: BACP).

Bradley, L. J. & Gould, L. J. (2001) 'Psychotherapy-based Models of Counselor Supervision' in Bradley, L. & Ladany, N. (eds) *Counselor Supervision: Principles, Process and Practice*, 3rd edn (Philadelphia, PA: Brunner-Routledge), pp. 147–175.

Carroll, M. (2004) *Counselling Supervision: Theory, Skills and Practice* (London: Sage).

Clarkson, P. (2002) *The Transpersonal Relationship in Psychotherapy* (London: Whurr).

Cooper, M. (2011) 'Meeting the Demand for Evidence Based Practice' *Therapy Today*, 22 (4), 10–16.

Cooper, M. & McLeod, J. (2010) 'Pluralism: Towards a New Paradigm for Therapy' *Therapy Today*, 21 (9).

'COPE' Therapeutic Picture Cards produced by OH-Publishing (www.oh-cards.com).

Copeland, S. (2005) *Counselling Supervision in Organisations* (London: Routledge).

Craib, I. (1994) *The Importance of Disappointment* (London: Routledge).

De Board, R. (1990) *The Psychoanalysis of Organisations* (London: Tavistock Publications, Routledge).

Department of Health (2011) *Talking Therapies: A Four Year Plan of Action*, www.dh.gov.uk/prod_consum_dh/groups/dh_digitalassets/documents/digitalasset/dh_123985.pdf, accessed 18 September 2012.

Despenser, S. (2011) 'What is Supervision?' *BACP Information Sheet (S2)* (Lutterworth: BACP).

Eiden, B. (1998) 'The Use of Touch in Psychotherapy' *Self and Society*, 26 (2), 3–8.

Feltham, C. & Dryden, W. (1994) *Developing Counselling Supervision* (London: Sage).

Gabriel, L. & Casemore, R. (2010) 'Guidance for Ethical Decision Making: A Suggested Model for Practitioners' *BACP Information Sheet (P4)* (Lutterworth: BACP).

Garbutt, L. (2009) 'Managing Psychotherapeutic Practice Between External Supervision Sessions: Understanding and Using the Concept of an Internal Supervisor' *Unpublished Doctoral Project* (Middlesex University).

Gendlin, E. (1979) *Focusing* (New York: Everest House).

Gilbert, M. & Evans, K. (2000) *Psychotherapy Supervision: An Integrative Relational Approach to Psychotherapy Supervision* (Buckingham: Open University Press).

Goldberg, C. (1981) 'The Peer Supervision Group: An Examination of its Purpose and its Process' *Group*, 5, 27–40 in Carroll, M. (2004) *Counselling Supervision: Theory, Skills and Practice* (London: Sage).

Goss, S. (2000) 'A Supervisory Revolution? The Impact of New Technology' in Lawson, B. & Feltham, C. (eds) *Taking Supervision Forward: Enquiries and Trends in Counselling and Psychotherapy* (London: Sage), pp. 175–189.

Hawkins, P. & Shohet, R. (2012) *Supervision in the Helping Professions*, 4th edn (Maidenhead: Open University Press).

Health Education Authority UK (HEA) (2000) *World Mental Health Day*, www.1stwebsite.com/hea/mentallhealth/intro.htm, accessed 20 November 2000.

Henderson, P. (2009) *A Different Wisdom: Reflections on Supervision Practice* (London: Karnac Books Ltd).

Henton, I. & Midgley, N. (2011) 'The Marriage of Practice and Science' *Therapy Today*, 22 (7), 26–27.

Her Majesty's Stationery Office (HMSO) (2010) *No Health without Mental Health*, www.dh.gov.uk/prod_consum_dh/groups/dh_digitalassets/documents/digital asset/dh_124058.pdf, accessed 18 September 2010.

Honey, P. & Mumford, A. (1993) *The Manual of Learning Styles*, 3rd edn (Maidenhead: Peter Honey Publications).

Inskipp, F. & Proctor, B. (2009) *Making the Most of Supervision*, 2nd edn (Twickenham: Cascade).

Izzard, S. (2001) 'The Responsibility of the Supervisor Supervising Trainees' in Wheeler, S. & King, D. (eds) *Supervising Counsellors: Issues of Responsibility* (London: Sage), pp. 75–92.

Jackson, C. (2012) 'Diagnostic Disarray' *Therapy Today*, 23 (3), 4–8.

Jacobs, M. (1996) *In Search of Supervision* (Buckingham: Open University Press).

Jacobs, M. (2007) 'Dual Roles – Blurring the Boundaries in Professional Relationships' *BACP Information Sheet (G3)* (Lutterworth: BACP).

Jenkins, P. (2007) *Counselling, Psychotherapy and the Law* (London: Sage).

Jesper, C. (2010) 'An Exploration into the Impact of Dual Relationships in Counselling Supervision' *Unpublished MA Dissertation* (Leeds Metropolitan University).

Jones, G. & Stokes, A. (2009) *Online Counselling: A Handbook for Practitioners* (Basingstoke: Palgrave Macmillan).

Kaberry, S. (2000) 'Abuse in Supervision' in Lawton, B. & Feltham, C. (eds) *Taking Supervision Forward: Enquiries and Trends in Counselling and Psychotherapy* (London: Sage), pp. 42–59.

King, D. (2001) 'Clinical Responsibility and the Supervision of Counsellors' in Wheeler, S. & King, D. (eds) *Supervising Counsellors: Issues of Responsibility* (London: Sage), pp. 7–21.

King, J. (2004) *Cellular Wisdom: Decoding the Body's Secret Language* (Berkeley: Ten Speed Press).

Kolb, D. A. (1984) *Experiential Learning* (Englewood Cliffs, NJ: Prentice-Hall).

Kübler-Ross, E. (1969) *On Death and Dying* (London: Routledge).

Ladany, N. & Bradley, L. J. (2010) *Counselor Supervision*, 4th edn (New York: Routledge).

Lago, C. (2006) *Race, Culture and Counselling: The On-going Challenge*, 2nd edn (Berkshire: Open University Press).

Lago, C. & Wright, J. (2007) 'E-mail Supervision' in Tudor, K. & Worrall, M. (eds) *Freedom to Practise Volume II: Developing Person-Centred Approaches to Supervision* (Ross-on-Wye: PCCS Books), pp. 102–118.

Lahad, M. (2002) *Creative Supervision: The Use of Expressive Arts Methods in Supervision and Self-Supervision* (London: Jessica Kingsley Publishers).

Langs, R. (1994) *Doing Supervision and Being Supervised* (London: Karnac Books Ltd).

Lawton, B. (2000) 'A Very Exposing Affair: Explorations in Counsellors' Supervisory Relationships' in Lawton, B. & Feltham, C. (eds) *Taking Supervision Forward: Enquiries and Trends in Counselling and Psychotherapy* (London: Sage), pp. 25–41.

Lawton, B. & Feltham, C. (eds) (2000) *Taking Supervision Forward: Enquiries and Trends in Counselling and Psychotherapy* (London: Sage).

Littrell, J. M., Lee-Borden, N. & Lorenz, J. A. (1979) 'A Developmental Framework for Counseling Supervision' *Counselor Education and Supervision*, 19, 119–136.

Loganbill, C., Hardy, E. & Delworth, U. (1982) 'Supervision: A Conceptual Model' *The Counselling Psychologist*, 10, 3–42.

London, Z. & Chester, A. (2000) 'Less Assessment and More Suggestions Please: Factors Contributing to Effective Supervision of Counsellors at Different Experience Levels' *Australian Social Work*, 53 (4), 47–53.

London School of Economics (LSE) (2012) *How Mental Illness Loses out in the NHS*, http://cep.lse.ac.uk/pubs/download/special/cepsp26.pdf, accessed 18 September 2012.

Martin, C., Godfrey, M., Meekums, B. & Madhill, A. (2011) 'Managing Boundaries Under Pressure: A Qualitative Study of Therapists' Experiences of Sexual Attraction in Therapy' *Counselling and Psychotherapy Research*, 11 (4), 248–256.

Maslow, A. H. (1943) 'A Theory of Human Motivation' *Psychological Review*, 50 (4), 370–396.

McLeod, J. (2008) 'Outside the Therapy Room' *Therapy Today*, 19 (4), 14–18.

McLeod, J. (2010) *Case Study Research in Counselling and Psychotherapy* (London: Sage).

Mearns, D. (2008) 'How Much Supervision Should You Have?' *BACP Information Sheet (S1)* (Lutterworth: BACP).

Mearns, D. & Cooper, M. (2005) *Working at Relational Depth* (London: Sage).

Menzies, I. E. P. (1979) 'Functioning of Social Systems as a Defence Against Anxiety' Centre for Applied Social Research (London: Tavistock Institute of Human Relations) cited in De Board, R. (1990) *The Psychoanalysis of Organisations* (London: Tavistock Publications, Routledge).

Merry, T. (1999) *Learning and Being in Person-Centred Counselling* (London: Sage).

Mitchell, B. & Bond, T. (2008) *Confidentiality and Record Keeping in Counselling and Psychotherapy* (London: Sage).

Mitchell, B. & Bond, T. (2010) *Essential Law for Counsellors and Psychotherapists* (London: Sage).

Mitchell, B. & Bond, T. (2011) *Legal Issues Across Counselling & Psychotherapy Settings: A Guide for Practice* (London: Sage).

Morrisey, J. & Tribe, R. (2001) 'Parallel Process in Supervision' *Counselling Psychology Quarterly*, 14 (2), 103–110.

Page, S. & Wosket, V. (2001) *Supervising the Counsellor: A Cyclical Model*, 2nd edn (London: Routledge).

Palmer, S. & Woolfe, R. (eds) (2000) *Integrative and Eclectic Counselling and Psychotherapy* (London: Sage).

Proctor, B. (1997) 'Supervision: Competence, Confidence and Accountability' *British Journal of Guidance and Counselling*, 22 (3), 309–319.

Proctor, B. (2008) *Group Supervision: A Creative Guide to Supervision*, 2nd edn (London: Sage).

Ricketts, T. & Donohoe, G. (2000) 'Clinical Supervision in Cognitive-Behavioural Psychotherapy' in Lawton, B. & Feltham, C. (eds) *Taking Supervision Forward: Enquiries and Trends in Counselling and Psychotherapy* (London: Sage), pp. 126–141.

Rosenberg, M. & Ronen, T. (1998) 'Clinical Supervision from the Standpoint of Cognitive-Behavioural Therapy' *Psychotherapy: Theory, Research, Practice, Training*, 35, 220–230.

Roth, A. D. & Pilling, S. (2008) *Supervision Competences Framework*, www.ucl.ac.uk/clinical-psychology/CORE/supervision_framework.htm, accessed 3 March 2013.

Rothschild, B. (2006) *Help for the Helper: The Psychophysiology of Compassion Fatigue and Vicarious Trauma* (London: W.W. Norton & Co.).

Rowan, J. (1993) *The Transpersonal: Psychotherapy and Counselling* (London: Routledge).

Schultz, W. C. (1989) *Joy* (Berkeley, CA: Science and Behavior Books).

Searles, H. F. (1955) 'The Informational Value of the Supervisor's Emotional Experience' *Psychiatry*, 18, 135–146 in Sumerel, M. (1994) *Parallel Process in Supervision* (Greensboro, NC: ERIC Digests).

Shohet, R. (ed.) (2008) *Passionate Supervision* (London: Jessica Kingsley Publishers).

Shohet, R. (ed.) (2011) *Supervision as Transformation: A Passion for Learning* (London: Jessica Kingsley Publishers).

Shuck, C. & Wood, J. (2011) *Inspiring Creative Supervision* (London: Jessica Kingsley Publishers).

Singh, H. & Boyle, M. (2004) 'Interhemispheric Interaction During Global-Local Processing in Mathematically Gifted Adolescents, Average Ability Youth and College Students' *Neuropsychology*, 18 (2), 371–377.

Smith, K. L. (2009) *A Brief Summary of Supervision Models*, www.gallaudet.edu/Documents/Academic/COU_SupervisionModels[1].pdf, accessed 13 March 2013.

Sperry, R. W. (1980) 'Mind–Brain Interaction: Mentalism, Yes: Dualism, No' *Neuroscience*, 5 (2), 195–206.

Stoltenberg, C. D. & Delworth, U. (1987) *Supervising Counselors and Therapists* (San Francisco: Jossey-Bass).

The Guardian (2010) 'UK Happiness Index to Gauge National Mood' The Guardian, Monday 15 November 2010, p. 1.

Topham, P. (2012) 'The Future is Appy' *Therapy Today*, 23 (3), 14–18.

Totton, N. (2005) *New Dimensions in Body Psychotherapy* (Maidenhead: Open University Press).

Totton, N. (2010) *The Problem with Humanistic Therapies* (London: Karnac Books Ltd).

Traynor, W. (2007) 'Supervising a Therapist Through a Complaint' in Tudor, K. & Worrall, M. (eds) *Freedom to Practise Volume II: Developing Person-Centred Approaches to Supervision* (Ross-on-Wye: PCCS Books), pp. 154–168.

Tuckman, B. W. (1965) 'Developmental Sequences in Small Groups' *Psychological Bulletin*, 63 (6), 384–399.

Tuckman, B. & Jensen, M. (1977) 'Stages of Small Group Development Revisited' *Group and Organisational Studies*, 2, 419–427.

Tudor, K. (2007) 'Group Supervision' in Tudor, K. & Worrall, M. (eds) *Freedom to Practise Volume II: Developing Person-Centred Approaches to Supervision* (Ross-on-Wye: PCCS Books), pp. 85–101.

Tudor, K. & Worrall, M. (eds) (2004) 'Person-Centred Philosophy and Theory in the Practice of Supervision' in Tudor, K. & Worrall, M. (eds) *Freedom to Practise: Person-Centred Approaches to Supervision* (Ross-on-Wye: PCCS Books), pp. 11–30.

Tudor, K. & Worrall, M. (eds) (2007) *Freedom to Practise Volume II: Developing Person-Centred Approaches to Supervision* (Ross-on-Wye: PCCS Books).

Tune, D. (2005) 'Dilemmas Concerning the Ethical Use of Touch in Psychotherapy' in Totton, E. N. (ed.) *New Dimensions in Body Psychotherapy* (Maidenhead: Open University Press), pp. 70–83.

UKCP (2012) *Information for the Public*, www.psychotherapy.org.uk/public.html, accessed 10 October 2012.

Valentine, J. (2004) 'Personal and Organisational Power: Management and Professional Supervision' in Tudor, K. & Worrall, M. (eds) *Freedom to Practise: Person-Centred Approaches to Supervision* (Ross-on-Wye: PCCS Books), pp. 115–131.

Vallance, K. (2004) 'Exploring Counsellor Perceptions of the Impact of Counselling Supervision on Clients' *British Journal of Guidance and Counselling*, 32 (4), 559–574.

Walker, M. & Jacobs, M. (2004) *Supervision Questions and Answers for Counsellors and Therapists* (London: Whurr).

Weaks, D. (2002) 'Unlocking the Secrets of "Good Supervision": A Phenomenological Exploration of Experienced Counsellors Perceptions of Good Supervision' *Counselling and Psychotherapy Research*, 2 (1), 33–39.

Webb, A. (2000) 'What Makes it Difficult for the Supervisee to Speak?' in Lawton, B. & Feltham, C. (eds) *Taking Supervision Forward: Enquiries and Trends in Counselling and Psychotherapy* (London: Sage), pp. 60–73.

Webb, A. & Wheeler, S. (1998) 'How Honest Do Counsellors Dare to Be in the Supervisory Relationship?' *British Journal of Guidance and Counselling*, 26, 509–524.

Wheeler, S. (2001) 'Supervision of Counsellors Working Independently in Private Practice: What Responsibility Does the Supervisor Have for the Counsellor and their Work?' in Wheeler, S. & King, D. (eds) *Supervising Counsellors: Issues of Responsibility* (London: Sage), pp. 110–130.

Wheeler, S. & King, D. (eds) (2001) *Supervising Counsellors: Issues of Responsibility* (London: Sage).

Wheeler, S. & Richards, K. (2007) 'The Impact of Clinical Supervision on Counsellors and Therapists, their Practice and their Clients: A Systematic Review of the Literature' *Counselling & Psychotherapy Research*, 7 (1), 54–65.

Wosket, V. (1999) *The Therapeutic Use of Self: Counselling Practice, Research and Supervision* (London: Routledge).

Index